Bridging Gaps

Implementing Public-Private Partnerships to Strengthen Early Education

Sarah Taylor Vanover, EdD

www.gryphonhouse.com

Copyright

© 2024 Sarah Taylor Vanover

Published by Gryphon House, Inc.
P. O. Box 10, Lewisville, NC 27023
800.638.0928; 877.638.7576 [fax]
Visit us on the web at www.gryphonhouse.com.

All rights reserved. No part of this publication may be reproduced or transmitted in any form or by any means, electronic or technical, including photocopy, recording, or any information storage or retrieval system, without prior written permission of the publisher. Printed in the United States. Every effort has been made to locate copyright and permission information.

Cover images used under license from Shutterstock.com.

Library of Congress Control Number: 2023945471

BULK PURCHASE

Gryphon House books are available for special premiums and sales promotions as well as for fund-raising use. Special editions or book excerpts also can be created to specifications. For details, call 800.638.0928.

DISCLAIMER

Gryphon House, Inc., cannot be held responsible for damage, mishap, or injury incurred during the use of or because of activities in this book. Appropriate and reasonable caution and adult supervision of children involved in activities and corresponding to the age and capability of each child involved are recommended at all times. Do not leave children unattended at any time. Observe safety and caution at all times.

This book is not intended to give legal or financial advice. All financial and legal opinions contained herein are from the personal research and experience of the author and are intended as educational material. Seek the advice of a qualified legal advisor or financial advisor before making legal or financial decisions.

Dedication

This book is dedicated to my colleagues Mike Hammons, Lauren Hogan, and Mandy Marler, who have shown me by example how to be a dedicated and outspoken advocate for young children.

Table of Contents

vii	**INTRODUCTION**	
1	**CHAPTER 1:**	The Child-Care Crisis in the United States
8	**CHAPTER 2:**	Structure of State-Funded Preschools
16	**CHAPTER 3:**	Structure of Federally Funded Preschool Programs: Head Start and Early Head Start
25	**CHAPTER 4:**	Structure of Private Child-Care Programs
37	**CHAPTER 5:**	A Possible Solution: Mixed-Delivery Care
48	**CHAPTER 6:**	Public-Private Partnerships
67	**CHAPTER 7:**	State Models of Mixed-Delivery Early Childhood Education
81	**CHAPTER 8:**	Universal Preschool Compared to Mixed-Delivery Care
91	**CHAPTER 9:**	Special Education and Mixed Delivery
98	**CHAPTER 10:**	Professional Development in a Mixed-Delivery Early Education System
106	**CHAPTER 11:**	Pay Parity for Early Educators and How Mixed Delivery Can Help
114	**CHAPTER 12:**	Planning and Implementing a Mixed-Delivery Early Childhood System
121	**CHAPTER 13:**	Contracts and Legal Partnerships
131	**CHAPTER 14:**	Next Steps: Advocating for Mixed-Delivery Care
138	**REFERENCES AND RECOMMENDED READING**	
146	**INDEX**	

Introduction

This book follows up on my first book, *America's Child-Care Crisis: Rethinking an Essential Business* (2021), which outlines the challenges that child-care programs, early education professionals, and the families they serve are facing. In this book, I offer a deeper exploration of a possible solution to the current crisis: a mixed-delivery care model to early childhood education. To better understand how mixed-delivery care works, we first need to have a good understanding of how three main models of preschool are structured (the next three chapters in this book) and their limitations. The remainder of the book defines mixed delivery in depth, analyzes how it is already being used in parts of the country, and determines what the steps for implementation would be to move forward. Once policy makers and administrators understand how each separate system works, it is important to show how each system can improve by sharing their best features with one another to increase family choice and financially stabilize the early education system.

HOW THIS BOOK IS ORGANIZED

Chapter 1 explains the current child-care crisis in the United States and outlines the steps in a call to action. Chapters 2 through 4 explain the problems with the current fragmented approach to child care, including state-funded, federally funded, and private models. Chapters 5 through 7 explore what the mixed-delivery system is and how it works in different settings. Chapter 8 explains how universal preschool and mixed-delivery care differ and describes the effects of universal preschool on funding. Chapter 9 covers the laws related to implementation of inclusive care in early childhood. Chapter 10 discusses the professional development needed and the implications for stakeholders in mixed-delivery care. Chapter 11 looks at possible solutions for educator compensation. Chapters 12 and 13 walk through the details of creating mixed-delivery partnerships. Chapter 14 outlines ideas for advocacy for mixed-delivery care.

CHAPTER 1

The Child-Care Crisis in the United States

Child care supports every industry in our nation, but it continues to have an unstable infrastructure. Child care was fragile long before the COVID-19 pandemic began, but after mandatory closures, reduced adult-to-child ratios in an effort to limit illness, and a significant workforce shortage, many child-care programs are on the brink of closure (Haspel, 2022).

A MODEL OF FINANCIAL INSTABILITY

The current child-care model in the United States isn't working. Families are the primary funding source for child care throughout the country; however, they cannot afford the true cost of child care. The full cost of services for a child's enrollment includes salary and benefits for each staff member who interacts with the child, fixed expenses such as rent and utilities, liability insurance for the program, food for meals and snacks, consumables such as art materials and cleaning supplies, and building and playground maintenance.

If each family had to pay their equal portion of all these expenses, child care would cost double or triple the rates that families currently pay. Because most families do not have the capacity to finance that type of expense, the cost of child care is subsidized by the salaries provided to the staff members. This means that many full-time child-care employees make so little money that they qualify for many government subsidies in order to care for their own families. It may also mean that child-care staff members do not earn enough money to send their own children to the facilities in which they work.

Although most child-care program owners would love to pay their staff members more, it is hard to continue raising the cost of care for families and expect them to continue to enroll their children. Child care is one of the few industries where supply-and-demand principles do not work. Many areas of the United States are considered child-care deserts, meaning that there is not enough available child care for the families who need to find care for their children. Although there is a demand for more quality care, entrepreneurs are not opening more child-care programs—whether in centers or in family child-care homes—due to the great risk of losing money or having to close their new businesses. These desert areas also show that certain populations of children, such as children with disabilities, children experiencing homelessness, and children from minority families, may have even less access to child care than the majority demographics in their areas.

When children do not have access to safe, high-quality child care, parents must make the tough decision to stay home and care for their children. That could mean that one adult is supporting an entire household on a small income. In other cases, it may mean that the family has no source of income and must apply for government subsidies to cover the costs of consistent housing, a stable food source, reliable transportation, and necessary medical care. Ultimately, the goal is for the adults in the home to have reliable jobs that can provide for the family, and that goal requires child care.

From the perspective of the business community, it can be a waste of resources to lose a qualified and valuable employee due to a lack of consistent child care. During a workforce shortage when each business has vacant positions, child care can be one of the major reasons that skilled adults are not applying for positions in their preferred field. Unstable child care can cause parents to miss work regularly, drop from full-time to part-time status, decline a promotion, or leave a position entirely. A lack of child care during evenings and weekends can prevent hospitals, manufacturers, retailers, or restaurants from obtaining necessary staff. The business community has as much of a vested interest in child care as many family members do.

Ultimately, this is a problem that affects a huge portion of the populace, so the nation needs to begin to address the issue.

A CALL TO ACTION

No single solution will solve the problem; however, there are possible solutions that can address the current child-care crisis. In 2021, I wrote *America's Child-Care Crisis: Rethinking an Essential Business* (Vanover, 2021) because COVID-19 highlighted and exacerbated the challenges of the already fragile child-care ecosystem in the United States. I concluded *America's Child-Care Crisis* with a call to action, which suggests in part:

- Paying early childhood educators a competitive wage
- Prioritizing the growth of family child-care homes
- Getting business buy-in
- Ensuring that all children have equal access to a high-quality child-care environment
- Disbursing public funding into private child-care programs to improve their financial stability

Each of these actions addresses problems within the child-care community that need to be resolved to strengthen child-care infrastructure and make sure that families who need quality child care have access to it.

PAYING EARLY CHILDHOOD EDUCATORS A COMPETITIVE WAGE

The most powerful way that the community can show respect to early childhood educators and demonstrate the value of the industry is to begin paying the early childhood workforce a competitive wage. If early childhood educators can work a full-time job and still qualify for a government subsidy, then clearly their contribution to working families and to growing healthy young children is not properly acknowledged. There should not be a significant wage gap between qualified kindergarten teachers, preschool teachers, and infant/toddler teachers. There must be a way to raise up the educators devoting their careers to preparing young children to become our future workforce.

Different states are finding innovative ways to increase salaries and enlarge the workforce. Some states have implemented wage-supplement programs that can provide additional stipends on top of what private child-care programs are already paying their staff members (Urban Institute, 2022). Other states are waiving the cost of child care for child-care employees' own children in an attempt to make their wages competitive with those in other industries (Loewenberg, 2022). These innovative practices will be essential to attract and retain qualified teachers to be a part of the early childhood education system.

PRIORITIZING THE GROWTH OF FAMILY CHILD-CARE HOMES

For many reasons, the number of family child-care homes in the United States has decreased significantly during the past ten to fifteen years (Child Care Technical Assistance Network, 2020). One predominant factor is the retirement of a generation of early childhood educators who also became small-business owners by running a child-care program in their homes. Other contributing factors are found in bureaucracy, such as local zoning laws that may prevent a small business from operating in a residential area.

Whatever the reason for the decrease in numbers, family child-care homes play an essential role in many communities. First, many families may not want to take an infant or young toddler to a large child-care center; a family child-care home is a smaller, more personal environment that may be more inviting to some families. Home-based care can also be a safer environment for children who are medically fragile or who have a developmental delay that causes them to feel overwhelmed in larger groups. Finally, family child-care homes offer families a cozier environment where siblings have the opportunity to be together (Weisenfeld and Frede, 2021).

Family child-care homes can be greatly beneficial in small, rural communities where homes may be spaced far apart from one another. A child-care center may not be able to attract enough families to travel a large distance to attend, but a family child-care home may need only three to five families to reach full enrollment. Also, family child-care homes have a great deal more flexibility for their hours of operation. Many can offer evening and weekend hours without having to find additional staff who are willing to work during that time frame. Parents may also feel more comfortable placing their children in a family child-care home for nighttime care because it may feel more like their own home than a child-care center. Family child-care homes can also be an important vehicle for child care in states where the cost of commercial property is too expensive for the typical child-care program.

To grow the number of family child-care homes throughout the country, states need to make active efforts to recruit and mentor child-care providers who also want to become small-business owners. This may require states to offer start-up funding for potential family child-care homes. Local communities need to be aware that family child-care homes are not like normal storefront businesses, and zoning regulations should not prohibit them from opening in a residential area. Also, local zoning fees should not be cost prohibitive for child-care providers. Many child-care providers have a degree or certificate in early education, but they may not have had business training. States need to provide training programs for family child-care providers to learn about budgeting, marketing, meeting regulations, and preparing taxes for their small business. These small steps may help increase child-care access throughout the state, but especially in rural areas or during non-traditional hours of operation.

GETTING BUSINESS BUY-IN

The business community is slowly becoming aware that increased access to child care is a benefit that employees may value just as much as paid leave or health insurance. Plus, with families having children later than in previous generations, an employee may have worked for the company for years and may have become a valuable asset before deciding to become a parent. At that point, the company has a vested interest in retaining the employee after the child arrives.

Due to the varying sizes of businesses and different age ranges of employees, not every employer needs to provide on-site child care for its employees. An employer should conduct a needs assessment to understand what the child-care needs are and how to support employees with young children. On-site child care is a huge benefit for a larger company, but it is not the only opportunity that employees may appreciate. Many employees may want to keep their children in a program that they have previously selected, so a monthly stipend toward employee child care may give staff the support they need while still allowing the families to choose the program that is best for their children. Other businesses may create an agreement with one or more local child-care programs to prioritize the enrollment of their employees and offer them a slight discount for their tuition; in return, the employer will compensate the child-care program for this consideration for its employees.

Whatever type of child-care support is offered, it is important for the employer to remember that employees have lots of different job opportunities, and a benefit such as child-care support may be the difference in a potential employee's selecting one business over another.

ENSURING THAT ALL CHILDREN HAVE EQUAL ACCESS TO HIGH-QUALITY CHILD CARE

All children should have equal access to high-quality child care, regardless of race, ethnicity, disability, or the family's ability to pay. When a child-care program is operating on a minimal budget, it can be overwhelming to support a child with challenging behaviors. Whether the behaviors come from a diagnosed disability, experience with previous trauma, a medical condition, or a different special need, child-care programs may not have the resources to support a child in the way that she needs. This means that many children may bounce from one child-care program to another as centers tell the family that they don't have the ability to support the child. In small communities with only a single program available, a family may not have lots of choices for child care. Centers that do support children who exhibit a variety of behaviors and have special needs may be well out of the price range of many working families.

Every child should have the opportunity to access a safe, high-quality child-care program. Head Start works hard at making sure that families living in poverty can access high-quality care, but many Head Start programs only offer half-day care (Office of Head Start, 2022). Also, most communities have a waiting list for available Head Start spots. Child-care subsidies may be able to cover part of the cost of child care, but the highest-quality programs usually charge more than the maximum subsidy rates. That weekly overage fee may be more than a family can afford and may prevent the child from attending a quality program.

Communities need to brainstorm ideas on how to develop high-quality child-care environments in all local neighborhoods. Philanthropies need to partner with nonprofit groups that can make sure young children have access to full-day child care for working families and not just three hours of care per day. Public school systems need to partner with local organizations to make sure that each elementary school has an after-school program for families who cannot leave work to pick their child up at 2:30 each afternoon. Developing access to care across communities will not only help more families participate in the workforce, but it will also prevent very young children from being left alone or supervised by only a slightly older sibling, options that could lead to accidents and injury.

MODELS OF EARLY CHILDHOOD EDUCATION IN THE UNITED STATES

The three main models of early childhood education in the United States are public school preschools, federally funded programs (Head Start and Early Head Start), and private child-care programs. Private programs can be either child-care centers or family child-care homes and are primarily funded by tuition paid by families. State-funded preschool and Head Start are financed through government funding. *Mixed-delivery* early childhood education entails a partnership between two of the three models to create a more enhanced early childhood experience (Early Care and Education Consortium, 2021).

DISBURSING PUBLIC FUNDING INTO PRIVATE CHILD-CARE PROGRAMS

Overlapping funding streams and disbursing public funding into the private child-care sector strengthen the current child-care system by allowing private child-care programs to receive a steady amount of income. Such additional funding also assists families who do not have their own means to pay for high-quality care. This type of financial arrangement would be considered a mixed-delivery early childhood system because a public early childhood program (such as a Head Start or state-funded preschool) would blend with a private early childhood system to benefit both parties.

CHAPTER 2

Structure of State-Funded Preschools

To understand the structure of state-funded preschool throughout the United States, we need to first understand what state-funded preschool is. Unlike private child-care programs that must follow state child-care licensing laws based on federal guidance, and unlike Head Start programs that must follow federal policy, states have a great deal of leeway on how to administer their state-funded preschool programs. This means that the quality of and access to state-funded programs vary widely. If the state is the only funding source, then the state can establish any regulations it wants to determine how the program is run. It is also up to the state to decide if it wants a state-funded preschool program at all. Several states that do not offer public school preschool programs instead use private child-care and Head Start programs for all their early childhood education programs.

WHAT QUALIFIES AS A STATE-FUNDED PRESCHOOL?

The National Institute for Early Education Research (NIEER) offers the best definition of what qualifies as state-funded preschool. Under NIEER's definition, a state-funded preschool program has these components:

- The program is funded, controlled, and administered by the state.
- The program serves preschool-aged children three to five years of age, particularly the two school years prior to kindergarten.
- The program's primary focus is early childhood education, not parent education.

- The program offers group learning at least twice a week.
- The state-funded preschool program is different from the state-subsidized child-care program. State-subsidized child care is federal funding disbursed through the state to help families with low incomes pay for child-care costs. State-funded preschool is the state's preschool program administered through the public school system.
- The program's primary focus does not have to be serving children with disabilities, but services for children with disabilities can be offered. (Friedman-Krauss et al., 2022)

Under this definition, the state can offer its program strictly within the public school system, or it can offer a mixed-delivery model to partner with private child-care programs and/or Head Start programs within the state. This definition also allows states to establish their own eligibility requirements based on income-level, diagnosed disabilities, or age.

TRENDS IN STATE-FUNDED PRESCHOOLS

NIEER provides an annual state-of-preschool report that looks at each state and territory in the United States and includes an individual report on each state as well as data on the country as a whole. According to the *2021 State of Preschool* report, in forty-four states and the District of Columbia, sixty-three preschool programs meet NIEER's definition of a state-funded preschool (some states have multiple preschool offerings) (Friedman-Krauss et al., 2022). Six states (Idaho, Indiana, Montana, New Hampshire, South Dakota, and Wyoming) do not offer state-funded preschool based on NIEER's definition. In addition, the *State of Preschool 2021* (Friedman-Krauss et al., 2022) report notes the following:

- 1,358,247 children in the United States are in state-funded preschool programs.
- 29 percent of four-year-olds are being served in state-funded preschool.
- 5 percent of three-year-olds are being served in state-funded preschool.
- 54 percent of children in low-income homes are not served in some type of early childhood education program (state-funded preschool, Head Start, or subsidized child care).

Despite the fact that the United States is serving well over 1 million children in state-funded preschools, it is only beginning to reach the children who need access to the service (Friedman-Krauss et al., 2022). Also, more than half of the children in families with lower incomes are still not receiving *any* type of early education, which is the prime reason for state-funded preschool in most states.

NIEER also tracks quality markers for the states that offer state-funded preschool. It bases the preschool program's quality on ten benchmarks (Friedman-Krauss et al., 2022):

1. Use developmental standards.
2. Use an approved curriculum.
3. Hire degreed teachers.
4. Have teachers who specialize in early childhood education.
5. Hire credentialed assistant teachers.
6. Have professional development requirements for staff.
7. Establish a maximum classroom size.
8. Establish an adult-to-child ratio for classrooms.
9. Have a screening and referral process.
10. Use continuous quality improvement.

When NIEER ranks the state preschool programs, each program receives a point for each quality benchmark. Very few programs receive a score of ten, and in 2021, fourteen states met fewer than 50 percent of the benchmarks. Some of the lowest-quality programs were, unfortunately, the biggest programs in the United States serving a large number of children. That meant that 38 percent of children enrolled in state-funded preschool throughout the United States were being served in a program that met less than 50 percent of the quality benchmarks (Friedman-Krauss et al., 2022). These benchmarks are designed to evaluate the programs at the state level, not at the individual program level. Of course, within each state, some programs are exemplary, and others need additional support to meet quality markers.

COMPONENTS OF STATE-FUNDED PRESCHOOLS

When state leaders sit down to design or revise their state-funded preschool program, they consider three main areas: resources, access, and quality. (Private child-care programs also have the same considerations, but unlike state-funded preschools that already have resources available, they must consider what income they can collect.)

RESOURCES

States typically have a budget in place with all the available resources that the state has to offer, but they must assess what resources need to be redirected toward preschool and whether there are any duplicative services that are already being offered to streamline the process.

States also need to consider what additional resources they can add to the preschool programs. If public school preschool programs also choose to become licensed childcare programs, these classrooms may also be able to use state subsidy dollars for families who have low incomes. If state-funded preschools collaborate with Head Start programs and meet both sets of requirements, they can receive both state and federal funds at the same time. These types of financial strategies can make the preschool programs more financially stable, and they can provide additional benefits for the families.

ACCESS

Access to early childhood education is one of the biggest issues to address when implementing an effective state-funded preschool program. The state administration must first determine whom they want to serve, which would be documented through eligibility requirements. If the state's main goal is to serve families with lower incomes, then it would put an income eligibility requirement into place. If the state wants to primarily serve children with disabilities, then it would add an eligibility requirement describing access to children with individualized education programs (IEPs). However, if the state wants to open the preschool program up to all preschool children, then it would list requirements only for age and state residency.

QUALITY

States must also consider the level of quality that they want for their preschool program while they are still in the planning process. They want to avoid the state-funded preschool option being viewed as the poorest quality, but that can occur if the per-child funding amount is too low or if too many children are placed in one classroom. NIEER's quality benchmarks have been a successful guiding tool for many states because they look at well-trained staff members, quality curriculum, health and safety of the classroom, and ways for the program to continue to improve after initial implementation (NIEER, 2021a). The NIEER benchmarks also correspond to the Individuals with Disabilities Education Act (IDEA) by aligning with the public school requirements for screenings and referrals for young children who may have a developmental delay.

Of course, most states cannot meet all ten benchmarks, so the state administrative team needs to look at the list of benchmarks and prioritize those they feel are the most important. For example, states may prioritize the degree and training of the lead teacher over the assistant teacher with the hope that the lead teacher will mentor the assistant teacher. Continuing professional development may not be as high a priority initially if the teacher already has a degree in early childhood education and has experience working with young children in another setting. Most states look at prioritizing health and safety factors (adult-to-child ratios and group sizes) and teacher qualifications first, knowing that the child's relationship with the teacher and the child's health and safety are the most important components for most parents (Vanover, 2016) and for liability reasons. To provide those key quality components, the state may have a limited eligibility, such as income eligibility requirements, and then gradually expand eligibility so that more students can participate. What each state should avoid is decreasing quality as eligibility increases. Offering a low-quality preschool program does not offer long-lasting benefits to children and families. In fact, participating in a low-quality preschool program could do more harm than good (Miranda, 2017).

CHALLENGES FOR STATE-FUNDED PRESCHOOLS

Many cities and states are considering universal pre-K as a way to help prepare children to be more successful in kindergarten and to make sure that underserved communities have access to the same resources as others. As states move forward to an expansion of state-funded preschool or even to a universal pre-K model, they need to consider the potential limitations of state-funded preschool to figure out how to best serve the children in their states. In the remainder of this chapter, we'll look at some of these challenges.

OFFERING CHILD CARE WHEN FAMILIES NEED IT

According to NIEER's *2021 State of Preschool* report, the daily schedule of state-funded preschools varied significantly among states: twenty-four states offered part-time preschool, fourteen offered school-day care, six offered extended day care, and seventeen determined the length of the school day at the local level. The school calendar also varied among states: one state offered preschool for the full calendar year, forty-five offered care for the school year, and seventeen let the local school districts determine the calendar (Friedman-Krauss et al., 2022). If the state offers only half-day preschool in the public school system to all children in the state, is it going to meet the needs of all families? If working families need care in the evening or on weekends, would weekday preschool eliminate time for the child to be with his family? Will families have choices regarding hours of operation for parents who work nontraditional hours?

DIFFERING ELIGIBILITY REQUIREMENTS AND ACCESS

Eligibility for child care is another characteristic that varies from state to state. With some states attempting to offer universal preschool—serving all preschool-aged children in the state or city in a free, quality preschool program—their eligibility requirements are going to be minimal. They may enroll children strictly based on age. Other states with more limited resources for state funding may impose additional eligibility requirements that limit the number of children who can enroll at one time. Currently, thirty-four states have income eligibility requirements to enroll in preschool (Friedman-Krauss et al., 2022). Some states also consider a child's diagnosis with a developmental delay as an eligibility criterion and offer them a priority slot (Friedman-Krauss et al., 2022).

Eligibility requirements drastically affect enrollment and participation. At least ten states serve less than 10 percent of eligible children with their preschool programs, and six states have enrollment of more than 70 percent of eligible children (Friedman-Krauss et al., 2022).

Eligibility is only one small step in providing access to state-funded preschool. Other factors include the following:

- Do families have a way to get their children to the program? Is it within typical driving distance or close to public transportation? How many enrollment slots are available within each district compared to the number of children who would be interested in attending the program?
- Do eligible families know the program exists and how to register for the program?
- Do the community preschool programs respect the cultural communities of the families they are serving? If the families do not feel comfortable with the way the programs are set up, what changes need to be made to make the classrooms more inviting to the families?
- Do the areas that have more families with lower incomes have access to high-quality preschool programs? Or, are there specific portions of the state that have no access to care (that is, are there child-care deserts)? For example, North Dakota offers its state-funded preschool program in only 33 percent of the school districts in the state (Friedman-Krauss et al., 2022). How can the state-funded preschool program make sure that more preschool classrooms are in those areas?

- Will all areas of the state offer the same level of preschool regardless of the community?
- Will the preschool programs participate in the Child and Adult Care Food Program or the National School Lunch Program so that low-income families have access to hot meals for their children during the school day?

When these barriers to enrollment are addressed, more families have access to child care and enrollment numbers will climb. In states where only 10–15 percent of eligible preschool students are enrolled in a state-funded preschool classroom, issues such as transportation, consumer education, staffing, and hours of operation often prevent families from taking advantage of the opportunity. These obstacles do not mean that a family does not want or need their children to be enrolled, but it could mean that specific barriers are preventing the family from enrolling. Each state needs to assess the areas of the community that have families with lower income, determine the needs of those communities, and then determine what resources need to be used.

STAFFING

Each year, NIEER analyzes how many states are meeting each of its ten benchmarks to determine which benchmarks are the most challenging to maintain. Looking at the sixty-six programs across Washington, DC, and the forty-four states, NIEER found the following in regard to teacher qualifications and training:

- Hire degreed teachers—36 programs
- Have teachers who specialize in early childhood education—51 programs
- Hire credentialed assistant teachers—19 programs
- Have professional development requirements for staff—18 programs (Friedman-Krauss et al., 2022)

As the early education industry faces a huge staffing crisis, it is not surprising that standards relating to teacher and assistant-teacher education and training seem the most difficult to meet. Many states can find lead teachers to meet the education requirements because the state may be able to pay a lead teacher slightly more than an assistant teacher. However, there is still a shortage of degreed teachers. During a large expansion or a shift to universal pre-K, the state preschool program may have difficulty finding trained staff, particularly in a mixed-delivery model where staff in child-care programs may not have completed credentials. In these cases, the state needs to determine a plan for a transition period to qualify additional staff members. For example, child-care programs that wish to participate in the mixed-delivery program may not initially have the trained staff members that are needed, but the state program may allow them a two- or three-year transition timeline to allow lead teachers to complete the necessary degrees or credentials. Other states have created a pathway for teachers who have a certain number of years of experience in the field and then have required new staff members to pursue the required education and credentials moving forward.

Once states have found a method of recruiting new teachers into the field, they must consider pay parity. This means parity with K–12 teachers, parity among teachers in the mixed-delivery system, and parity with jobs in other competitive fields. It also means parity in benefits, including paid time off and health care. If qualified teachers do not earn a salary that will allow them to support their own families, the state will not be able to retain the workforce it needs to run the preschool program.

FUNDING

According to the NIEER 2021 report, the average cost per child per year in state-funded preschool is $7,011, but states funded as little as $2,200 per child per year. Total state spending on preschool has doubled in the past two decades from $4.13 billion in 2002 to $8.98 billion in 2021 (without COVID aid), but the per-child amount did not significantly increase during that time (Friedman-Krauss et al., 2022). States are attempting to serve more children, but they are not necessarily increasing the quality for each child.

To receive additional—and continuous—funding, the state needs to collect copious data on who is being served in the preschool system and what services are being used. In relation to the children who attend preschool, the state needs to document the developmental increases that children experience when participating in the program, as well as child outcomes in elementary school and family outcomes. For example, anecdotal evidence can demonstrate how families are positively affected by their children's participation in preschool, such as a child with a disability being identified while attending preschool and receiving the support and therapy the child needed to enter kindergarten with more confidence. Program administrators need to continuously share these stories and data with legislators and the state's department of education to show the state's administration the power and reach of a successful state-funded preschool program. Those results and powerful stories can help to ensure that the state-funded preschool system is a permanent addition to the state instead of an educational fad.

CHAPTER 3

Structure of Federally Funded Preschool Programs: Head Start and Early Head Start

Influenced by research on the lifelong and educational impacts of poverty, President Lyndon B. Johnson declared his War on Poverty during his 1964 State of the Union Address (Office of Head Start, 2022). Johnson's War on Poverty included the birth of the Head Start program. In 1975, Head Start published the first Head Start Program Performance Standards to ensure both uniformity for all programs and the ability to serve children with fidelity. In 1995, the first Early Head Start programs were created to serve prenatal mothers and children from infancy through thirty-six months of age. Then, in 1998, the US Congress authorized Head Start to expand to full-day and full-year programs when needed. In 2011, the US Department of Health and Human Services (HHS) put into place the current accountability program with its Designation Renewal System (DRS) for programs to have a five-year grant renewal cycle (Office of Head Start, 2022). If programs do not meet mandatory criteria, they are not eligible to compete for the grant in the next cycle.

Head Start has an unusual federal-to-local funding model. Congress approves Head Start's annual funding for each year, and the funds come through the HHS Administration for Children and Families. Instead of passing through state government, the funds go directly to local grantees (Early Childhood Learning and Knowledge Center, 2023). Many different organizations can apply to be a local grantee, including public schools, nonprofits, for-profits, faith-based organizations, and community organizations.

Becoming a Head Start grantee involves a competitive application process that can take several years of applying before an organization is awarded a grant. When applying to be a grantee, the organization must show that it has community support and strong partnerships with other key partners in the area. The grant specifically focuses on serving children from birth to five, including prenatal services for pregnant mothers. The grantee also applies for a specific number of slots for the represented area. Those slots can be in multiple settings such as self-run facilities or partner child-care programs.

The grantee also designates how many Head Start/Early Head Start slots would be part of the grant (Early Childhood Learning and Knowledge Center, 2023). The grantee is responsible for filling each slot that is awarded, so the organization must have the capacity to get those classrooms and partnerships running by the time the grant period begins. Along with finding the children to fill each slot, the grantee must have the child-development staff members to work with children as well as additional staff members who focus on family supports.

ELIGIBILITY REQUIREMENTS AND FAMILIES SERVED

The goal of Head Start is to support families living in poverty, so the eligibility requirements focus on income eligibility (Early Childhood Learning and Knowledge Center, 2023). Families can qualify for Head Start and Early Head Start services if they have children between the ages of birth and five years old (or a pregnant mother) and:

- the family is at 100 percent of the federal poverty level (FPL) or below;
- the family participates in Temporary Assistance for Needy Families (TANF), Supplemental Security Income (SSI), or Supplemental Nutrition Assistance Program (SNAP);
- the child is in foster care or experiencing homelessness.

A small number of children can qualify even if they do not meet the eligibility requirements. For example, the Head Start Program Performance Standards allow for up to 10 percent of the enrollment slots to be used by children with disabilities (Early Childhood Learning and Knowledge Center, 2023).

Between Head Start and Early Head Start programs, more than one million children are served each year. In 2021, 27 percent of grantees served Head Start children, 12 percent served Early Head Start children, and 61 percent served children in both Head Start and Early Head Start. Ninety-seven percent of Head Start children served were in centers, but there were also children served by home visitors—teachers who visit the children weekly in their own homes (Early Childhood Learning and Knowledge Center, 2023).

PROGRAMS AND SERVICES PROVIDED

Based on the needs of the family and the age of the children, Head Start offers a variety of services to support children throughout the United States.

- **Center-based care:** The center-based option is most popular for Head Start and Early Head Start families. Most Head Start children and approximately two-thirds of Early Head Start children (and pregnant mothers) are served in the classrooms (Early Childhood Learning and Knowledge Center, 2023).

- **Home-based care:** Home-based services are delivered in the child's home on a weekly basis (Early Childhood Learning and Knowledge Center, 2023). The visits focus on establishing routines, developing positive parent-child interactions, and using household items for learning activities. The home-based programs also have monthly group socialization activities for a small group of children and their families who are participating in home-based learning.

- **Family child-care homes:** Along with larger child-care centers, Head Start and Early Head Start also provides services through family child-care homes (Early Childhood Learning and Knowledge Center, 2023). The family child-care homes offer the same high-quality learning environments and curriculum, but they also allow families the option of having their children in a smaller environment where siblings can be together during the birth-to-five age range.

- **Migrant and Seasonal Head Start:** This program focuses on families where the adults are migrant farm workers and may have to move depending on the crop season and the time of year (Early Childhood Learning and Knowledge Center, 2023). Depending on where the program is located, the calendar may be set up to follow the agricultural year instead of the school-year calendar. Migrant and Seasonal Head Start promotes a consistent and educational environment for children who may have to move from state to state throughout the calendar year.

- **American Indian and Alaska Native Head Start:** In 1965, Head Start piloted thirty-four programs specifically focused on American Indians and Alaska Natives, and now those programs have grown to serve more than 44,000 children

(Early Childhood Learning and Knowledge Center, 2023). American Indian and Alaska Native programs have a separate funding stream from the states in which the territories are located. These programs operate to support the specific cultural needs of their communities instead of the state at large.

Although all quality early childhood programs focus on supporting all areas of the child's development, Head Start programs take that charge one step further. These additional supports can be in place due to their federal funding streams that provide for more than a typical classroom education. Head Start focuses on health and family supports that can help the children and the family eventually break the poverty cycle.

- **Health services**—Children enrolled in a Head Start or Early Head Start program receive healthy meals and snacks while in attendance, and that includes providing infants with appropriate formula (Early Childhood Learning and Knowledge Center, 2023). Family services staff make sure that all children receive medical, dental, vision, hearing, and behavioral screenings, and then assist the family through the referral process if the screening shows that the child needs additional support. Head Start programs encourage proper oral health by helping children brush their teeth at school and providing dental care if it is needed. Children can even receive mental health supports if needed.
- **Family care**—Starting with prenatal care, Head Start makes sure that the family members also receive the care they need so they can care for their children (Early Childhood Learning and Knowledge Center, 2023). If a pregnant mother is having difficulty getting transportation to prenatal visits or obtaining vitamins during pregnancy, the family service workers can make sure that she gets the supports she needs for a healthy pregnancy. They can also assist parents with applying for government assistance programs to ensure the family has safe housing, a stable food source, and reliable transportation. As the child grows, Head Start programs can offer families parenting training so that parents have appropriate developmental expectations for their children. If the parents need assistance obtaining a job or completing a General Educational Development (GED) test, family resource staff can help the parent through these processes step by step.

TEACHER REQUIREMENTS

To ensure that Head Start and Early Head Start classrooms maintain high-quality learning environments, Head Start programs strive to hire the highest-quality staff in the early childhood education field. The Head Start Program Performance Standards

(HSPPS) outline the requirements for child-development staff to make sure that programs across the United States have high-quality teachers working with young children (Early Childhood Learning and Knowledge Center, 2023).

- A Head Start or Early Head Start program director must have a bachelor's degree and experience in staff supervision, fiscal management, and administration.
- The manager for child and family services staff must have a bachelor's degree, preferably in one of the supervisory areas, such as family, health, or disabilities.
- The manager for Head Start classrooms must have a bachelor's degree in early childhood education (or an equivalent field) and experience in teaching.
- Teachers in an Early Head Start classroom must have a minimum of a Child Development Associate (CDA) certificate.
- Teachers in a Head Start classroom must have a minimum of an associate's degree or a bachelor's degree in early childhood education or its equivalent. Also, a minimum of 50 percent of the teachers nationwide must have a bachelor's degree in the field.
- Head Start assistant teachers must have a minimum of a CDA certificate or a state certificate that surpasses the CDA credential.
- Family child-care providers must at least be enrolled in a family child-care CDA program (or the state equivalent) and complete the certificate within eighteen months of starting it.
- Home visitors must have a minimum of a home-based CDA credential and show competency in implementing home-based activities.

Along with a variety of education credentials, Head Start and Early Head Start programs offer continuous training for their staff members through attending professional development training and by sending technical assistance coaches into the classrooms to observe and mentor the teachers in real-life situations (Early Childhood Learning and Knowledge Center, 2023).

ACCOUNTABILITY PROCEDURES

At all times, Head Start programs must follow the HSPPS. If the programs are licensed by the state or are part of the public school system, then they must also be in compliance with those requirements. To make sure that programs receiving federal funds for Head Start are compliant, the Office of Head Start encourages a stringent system of continuous monitoring within each grantee's organization. This begins with technical assistance coaches observing and assessing classrooms using the Classroom Assessment Scoring System. Monitoring also includes education managers and Head Start directors conducting announced and unannounced visits to make sure that all programs are meeting the required objectives.

The Office of Head Start participates in the monitoring process as well. During the five-year grant period, the federal government will conduct on-site monitoring visits that cover areas such as the health and safety of classrooms, fiscal management, or audits of enrollment records. Programs with minor violations will be asked to correct those violations immediately. Programs with many violations may lose their ability to reapply for status as a grantee at the end of the five-year funding period. If the Head Start program has openings in a Head Start or Early Head Start partnership program, the supervising Head Start program is still responsible for maintaining full enrollment at those facilities even if there is separate management for the independent facility. The contract between the Head Start grantee and the partnership site should include mandatory compliance with all federal and state requirements such as the HSPPS. If the partner facility cannot maintain the requirements, then the grantee may need to consider ending the partnership.

COMMUNITY INVOLVEMENT

Head Start programs strive to create mutually respectful programs within communities to help children and families be successful (Early Childhood Learning and Knowledge Center, 2023). To give guidance to all Head Start programs on this topic, the Office of Head Start created the Head Start Parent, Family, and Community Engagement Framework (US Department of HHS, 2018). This framework specifically looks at the impact areas that can help create positive family and child outcomes. The framework also focuses on equity by being culturally and linguistically inclusive to support the most families possible.

Family engagement begins with inviting families into the classrooms, planning family events, offering parent education and job training, and offering parents supports such as assisting with benefit applications. Head Start also works toward starting with families and growing involvement toward more of the community. Events such as community gardening, job fairs, and international potlucks are activities that can begin to engage more than currently enrolled families.

Establishing positive relationships throughout the community is a huge help when family service workers go out into the community to recruit new families to enroll their children in Head Start or Early Head Start during the following school year. If a family feels safe with the organization, and the organization has a good reputation in the neighborhood, they are much more likely to enroll their children. If the family is skeptical and worried about a visit from social services or deportation risks, they are not going to feel safe leaving their children or even giving personal information so that they can go through the enrollment process.

Community partnerships can also be beneficial for other community stakeholders to see. If the public library, food pantry, or local homeless shelter sees the impact that the Head Start grantee is making in the neighborhood, they are much more likely to want to partner with the grantee and set up a shared-services network to streamline resources and efficiently serve each family. This same type of visible partnership can assist when the time comes for applying for larger community grants or getting letters of support during the reapplication process.

CHALLENGES FOR HEAD START

Although Head Start has a consistent funding stream through the federal government and an established standard of operation for all programs, it still faces barriers, just as the private child care and state-funded preschool sectors of early childhood education do.

TRANSPORTATION

One common barrier for Head Start enrollment is transportation (National Head Start Association [NHSA], 2022). Many Head Start programs try to have their own bus or to work out a contract with the public school system to share bus transportation for their students, but this is not possible for all programs. In urban areas, Head Start facilities may be close enough for families in the neighborhood without transportation to walk to the program. However, there are plenty of reasons, such as busy interstates and poor weather conditions, that could prevent foot transportation. In rural areas, families may be spaced so far apart that it is challenging to send a bus to pick up all children enrolled in the program.

Aside from the families' locations, insurance and maintenance of a school bus or fifteen-passenger van is extremely expensive, so smaller Head Start grantees may not have the funding to make this type of investment for their programs (NHSA, 2022). Considering the workforce shortage after the COVID-19 pandemic, school bus drivers have been hard to train and hire, much less keep on staff. Some Head Start programs have tried to offer commercial driver's license (CDL) training programs to parents looking for a job, thereby offering them a skill set and obtaining new bus drivers in the process. This effort worked in some communities, but other neighborhoods did not see interest.

LIMITED HOURS OF OPERATION

Head Start's traditional hours of operation are also somewhat limiting for families. Many Head Start classrooms still operate on a half-day schedule. If a parent or guardian is at home during the day, a three- or four-hour school day is not that challenging, but when families are attempting to work, it can be hard to have care for children for only a small portion of the day. If the Head Start program does not have some type of extended care, then the family would need to find an additional location to send the child for the remainder of the day or remove the child from the program completely. If the child leaves the Head Start program for alternative child care, they could also lose hot meals, necessary medical care, and mental health supports. Some grantees are limited to offering half-day services due to facility limitations, because they can serve twice as many children in the same building if they operate half-day classrooms. Other grantees may need additional staff or financial resources to offer full-day classrooms.

INFANT AND TODDLER CARE

Although many areas have Head Start programs, Early Head Start classrooms are still limited in number, and many families are searching for quality infant and toddler care (NHSA, 2022). This is often the time in the family's life that one or more members of the family decide to leave the workforce if there is no one who can care for an infant. Infants and toddlers can also be the most stressful for new parents. Not knowing how to soothe a crying baby can cause a huge increase in stress for families, and families living in poverty already experience a great deal of stress. An Early Head Start classroom can provide the parent with education on caring for a new baby and give the family a break from stress to improve quality of life for everyone in the home.

STAFFING

As with state-funded and private child-care programs, staffing in Head Start and Early Head Start is a major issue. Many Head Start programs are struggling to find qualified staff members due to workforce shortages (NHSA, 2022). A lack of staffing may limit the number of classrooms that the grantee can open and may change the number of slots in the grant. Again, Head Start can offer training programs and the CDA certificate to its staff members or interested parents who want job training. And because of the federal funds it receives, Head Start has the ability to pay more than typical private child-care programs can, but highly trained staff can often make a larger salary in the public school system. Also, since many

Head Start grantees are nonprofit organizations, staff benefits may also be better in the public school system. Once again, the staffing shortage speaks to the desperate need for a competitive salary and benefits in the field of early childhood education to make sure that skilled staff are working with young children when they are the most impressionable.

VISIBILITY

Many families simply do not understand the benefits of Head Start or understand that they are eligible because the program is not marketed to them in the way that is necessary. Programs such as Head Start grantees often have interactive websites that can explain the services they offer, but if the families don't know that Head Start is out there, they will not look for it.

Despite any challenges that Head Start programs may be facing with staffing or transportation plans, Head Start and Early Head Start classrooms consistently serve the most vulnerable children and families in the Unites States. They give children the opportunity to maximize their development, not only with high-quality classrooms but also with access to health and dental care, nutritious meals, and screenings for possible developmental delays. They give parents the opportunity to learn about child development and even to complete their own education so they can pursue higher-paying jobs. Even if these services are only offered for three to four hours per day in a half-day preschool classroom, they are services that many families cannot do without.

CHAPTER 4

Structure of Private Child-Care Programs

While the structure of Head Start programs remains relatively uniform, the structure of private child-care programs can vary from state to state and even within a community. Private child-care programs are basically small businesses with individual owners or administrative boards that must operate at or above the state's minimum child-care guidelines. These programs can be nonprofit or for-profit businesses. Many child-care programs register as nonprofit organizations so they can receive the financial discounts associated with nonprofit organizations. Regardless of how the business is registered (nonprofit or for-profit status), most child-care programs receive barely sufficient income to pay the monthly expenses.

If the minimum health and safety standards are met, then the owner of the program can decide which quality standards to implement. The federal government requires private child-care programs to meet some basic standards, such as staff background checks; however, the states also have a lot of freedom on what they can require the child-care programs in their area to do to meet the minimum standards for operation. In this chapter, we'll look at the general structure of private child-care programs.

FINANCIAL STRUCTURE

Private child-care programs are funded primarily by tuition paid by families and by child-care subsidies. Some programs may receive small amounts of funding through grants or donations; however, it is very hard to receive outside funding for general operations. Grants are usually dedicated to a specific project and not for general funding. Staff salaries are these programs' largest expense; other large expenses include mortgage or rent, utilities, insurance, food, and building maintenance.

TUITION

The reason that child-care programs are so financially fragile is because they are primarily parent funded. On average, parents spend approximately $42 billion per year on child care, significantly more than the investment by the federal government (Gould and Blair, 2020). In every state, federally funded opportunities are available to families for child-care subsidies, but those opportunities are for those with very low incomes. Many working families, particularly those with two adults working, do not qualify for subsidies and must pay for child care completely out of their own income. To attract families to their child-care programs, owners must set their tuition rates based on what families can afford instead of what it actually costs to run the program. This may mean surveying other successful programs in the area to see how much they charge and to determine whether they have a waiting list for available spots.

When a program chooses to voluntarily reduce the adult-to-child ratios in the classrooms to offer a higher quality of care, the program will lose tuition for the enrollment spots it is no longer offering. In turn, the program can charge slightly more for tuition since the families realize the care will be of a higher quality. Yet, even though the parents are willing to pay more for higher-quality care, the program may not be able to make up the full economic loss of the ratio change. Some families may leave the program because the new tuition may be more than they can afford. Increases in quality must still allow for the tuition to be affordable; otherwise, the business will not be able to survive.

CHILD-CARE SUBSIDIES

Every state has the opportunity to receive federal funding for child care from the Child Care and Development Block Grant (CCDBG) issued by the federal government. The state must provide a match to the federal funds to receive the money, and the block grant requires that basic health and safety requirements are demonstrated for any program that benefits from the federal funds (Office of Child Care, 2012). Even though the funds come from a block grant (which may be perceived as being rather flexible), some specific required percentages limit how the state spends the federal funds.

The block grant identifies high-priority groups—families with low income, children experiencing homelessness, children in foster care, and so on—that should receive subsidy for child care before the general public does (Office of Child Care, 2012). The grant also designates that 70 percent of the funds administered to individual states go toward direct services for families, which typically means the child-care subsidy program. Each state sets an eligibility level for families to enter the child-care subsidy program. For example, one state may determine that families must be at 200 percent of the Federal Poverty Level (FPL) or below to qualify for subsidy. After the state determines who can qualify for child-care subsidy, then the state determines what percentage of the child-care cost it is able to cover for each family. For example, a state may decide that families at or below 160% of the federal poverty level can qualify for child-care subsidy. Then, for the families who qualify, the state will cover the cost of child care at 60 percent of the market-rate value. That means that a family receiving subsidy can have the full cost of child care covered at 60 percent of the available programs, but if they choose one of the other 40 percent of child-care programs, they will have to pay a tuition balance due after the child-care subsidy has been paid.

Most states conduct a market-rate survey every two to three years to see what the average cost of care is for the child-care programs throughout the state. Based on what the programs in the state are charging, the state will decide how much it can cover. Perhaps the state can cover the full cost of child care at 60 percent of the programs in the state, but the families on subsidy will have to pay the balance at the 40 percent of the programs that are the most expensive. Paying a balance can be a great burden for some families. If there is a $60 balance per week for a child, a family may have to pay $240 per month in additional fees. If the family does not have that $240, they cannot attend that particular child-care program. Most families who use child-care subsidy must go to a center where the tuition is fully covered by the monthly subsidy. While having tuition fully covered is a relief for a family with low income, that may also mean that the family is unable to place their children in a high-quality child-care program that charges more than the state maximum subsidy rates.

Not all states are conducting a market-rate survey anymore. The federal government will allow states to do a research-based study to determine the cost of quality child care where the workers make a livable wage and the adult-to-child ratios are safe for the children (Office of Child Care, 2014). Once the cost-of-care study is complete, the state will determine the percentage of the cost that it can cover. This system pays a larger portion of child-care tuition for the families enrolled in the subsidy program; however, the state may not be able to serve as many families due to limited funds. The child-care programs would be reimbursed at a higher rate with this option, so centers would have the opportunity to pay their staff a higher wage and potentially keep staff members longer.

Aside from the direct funds that go to families in each state for child-care subsidies, the other funds from the block grant go toward infrastructure rather than directly toward programs. These funds are used to pay for quality systems such as the state's child-care licensing services and the state's quality rating system, which ranks the programs' quality levels for parents. States also use block grant funds to administer the child-care background check system and set up professional development for child-care providers throughout the state. Typically, a minority of families in each state receive some type of subsidy for their child-care costs, so this is why parents still finance the majority of child care in each state.

STAFF SALARIES

Staff salaries are the single largest—and most variable—expense for all child-care programs. Rent and electric bills are set by outside vendors, but the owner can determine how much to pay the staff members. Minimum-wage laws, federal law, and possibly state laws are the only guidelines that the employer must follow. But the local competition is also a driving factor for salaries. When other child-care programs are paying a higher wage, staff members may be compelled to leave one center and apply at another. Compared to other types of jobs, teachers may not want to leave the children and families they love, even if the wages are better at other businesses. Some child-care programs hope that the families and a positive work environment may be enough to keep employees at their programs.

Child-care programs are not just competing against one another for staff members. The retail industry and hospitality industry can offer many child-care providers higher wages, and employees do not have to take work home with them in those industries. Independent child-care programs often compete with Head Start programs and public school systems for teachers with higher education levels. With state and federal funding to support their programs, Head Start and state-funded pre-K can pay staff members a higher wage and often have more comprehensive benefits packages. Private child-care programs have a hard time providing benefits packages that can compete with a large business. One of the most common employee benefits that a child-care program can offer is a discount on child care for employees' children. This can be a great asset for a parent-employee who can be in the same building each day as their child and not have to pay for the full cost of care. At the same time, this discount is another example of how a child-care program loses income and must operate on a smaller budget.

TEACHER REQUIREMENTS

Teacher requirements for private child-care programs vary throughout the United States. The most basic requirements include making sure that the teacher is legally an adult, has a high school diploma or GED, and has the required annual training hours. Some states allow high school students to work in child-care programs, but they may not be able to work without the supervision of an adult because the background-check process for youth is not as extensive. Other states may have a higher level of training required to be a lead teacher or an assistant teacher in the classroom, but that requirement can potentially affect the program's ability to recruit staff if the program pays lower wages.

The federal government requires that all states offer a preservice training for new child-care providers entering the field. The training topics include basic health and safety requirements, the basics of CPR and first aid, and how to identify abuse and neglect. New child-care program staff, even those not working in the classroom, must complete the training within the first three months of working in child care. Child-care programs, whether in family child-care homes or in centers, must at all times have present staff who are currently certified in first aid and CPR.

After states identify the required training basics, they also have the option to increase the amount of mandated training topics so that each provider has training that the states deem necessary. Many states have added required training on topics such as trauma-informed care, special education, or other topics that may be a particular need within the state. Each state has some type of continuing professional-development training requirement. It may be an annual or a biennial requirement. Regardless of the time frame, all child-care providers must continue to learn new information in their profession to improve their skills for working with children and families.

SAFETY COMPONENTS

The largest concern for all child-care providers is keeping the children safe and healthy while they are apart from their families. Background checks are a first step for keeping children safe in all child-care settings, including private child-care programs. The federal government mandates a comprehensive background-check program for all child-care centers and family child-care homes that are regulated through the state (Office of Child Care, 2012). Child-care programs had already been required to have background checks on their employees, but the programs were required to do a background check only when a new employee was hired. After being hired, the employee could potentially commit a crime, and the child-care program would not know about it. This was a huge flaw in the previous system.

The new requirements, reaffirmed in 2023, also included a more comprehensive view of federal crimes, state crimes, and crimes listed in the sex offender database (Office of Child Care, 2012). Finally, each state's child-care background check system needed to find a way to communicate with other states in order for child-care program owners to learn whether a potential employee had committed a crime in another state. This new system was separate from the background-check system that many states use for their public school systems, and in some cases, the new system was far more comprehensive. The federal Office of Child Care viewed this change in the background check system as a foundation for the health and safety of children in regulated child care.

Another key part of keeping children healthy and safe is maintaining adult-to-child ratios and classroom sizes where adults can give the needed attention to each child in the classroom. The federal government does not mandate the ratios or the classroom size of private child-care programs; that decision is up to the state. However, the federal government does make sure that the state maintains the ratios that they have put into place. When the state sets the ratios, they consider:

- how many children are needed in each classroom to make sure that the center can maintain a profit, however small that may be;
- how many children an individual adult feels comfortable caring for at one time;
- how many children that research indicates as the best number for individualized learning; and
- how many children may have special needs and require additional attention.

In addition, the federal government requires that all child-care programs have procedures for disasters and emergencies. Emergency management plans include practicing drills for fire, tornadoes, earthquakes, and lockdowns, as well as planning for emergencies such as the COVID-19 pandemic. Another important safety concern is the correct administration of medication while a child is in attendance at a child-care program. States need to make sure that medication is secure, refrigerated (if needed), and administered at the correct time. Along with medication administered on a regular basis, all staff members need training on where the emergency medication is kept, which children may need it, and how to administer that type of medication if they are caring for the child when the child gets sick. Finally, all private child-care providers must understand mandatory reporting procedures for child abuse in their states. The federal government requires that all child-care providers be trained in identifying potential abuse, and this type of information must be included in each state's preservice training (Office of Child Care, 2014).

QRIS SYSTEM

Another federal requirement for each state's child-care system is to have a Quality Rating and Improvement System (QRIS). Most states have set this system up as a star-rated system, similar to the systems used by hotels. The higher quality the program, the more stars it will have. Child-care centers and family child-care homes can both be incorporated into these systems, but each state's system is individualized to the state's needs. Along with the actual star rating that the program receives, resources are available to assist with increasing quality. Child-care programs can receive technical assistance on meeting health and safety requirements, designing classrooms, attending professional development opportunities, or creating appropriate curriculum. As child-care programs receive more technical assistance, they have the opportunity to increase their star rating and move higher on the rating scale.

The rating scale can be beneficial for the child-care program because families in each state can search for the highest-rated programs as they look for a program for their children to attend. Participating in the QRIS is basically a type of advertising for the program to show that it is high quality. It can also be a goal to motivate programs to achieve a higher level of quality and receive additional recognition for their achievements. In most states, the QRIS system is for those programs that want to participate willingly (programs may choose not to participate). In other states, child-care programs must participate to receive any type of state or federal funding, such as participating in the state's child-care subsidy program. Most states simply encourage participation in the program with the hope that lower-rated programs will be motivated to increase their scores. In other states, the program may have a minimum score required to participate in additional funding opportunities.

CHALLENGES FOR PRIVATE CHILD-CARE PROGRAMS

Private child-care programs face huge hurdles, including funding, staffing issues, providing sufficient child care for families who work nontraditional hours, offering access to child care in rural communities, providing enough slots for infants and toddlers, and offering support for children with special needs.

FUNDING

Despite differences across state lines, all child-care programs seem to struggle financially. The cost of care is more than programs can actually charge the families enrolling their children, especially the youngest children. Infants have the lowest staff-to-child ratio because they have the highest level of need with the lowest level of independence. Depending on the state, one adult may be caring for three to five infants individually, and the maximum classroom size for infants is smaller than any other age group. Adult-to-child ratios increase with the child's age. A preschool classroom may have a ratio in which one teacher can care for ten to fourteen children on his own, since the students are more independent by the time they are three and four years old. The largest adult-to-child ratio in a child-care program is in a school-age program for children between kindergarten and middle school ages.

Child-care programs lose money on their infant classrooms. When one adult can watch only four children at a time, and additional teachers may be needed when multiple babies are fussy or need to eat at the same time, the cost of the staff is more expensive than the tuition that the program is bringing in for the children enrolled in the infant classroom. And, of course, a portion of every child's tuition is dedicated to pay for fixed expenses such as rent, utilities, administrative staff, insurance, and other services that occur outside of the classroom environment.

The loss of income is reduced in the toddler classroom because the ratio increases, and depending on what the child-care program charges, the center may begin to break even in the two-year-old classroom. The preschool classroom is the first classroom from which the center could potentially make money from enrollment. Although preschool tuition is discounted more than infant tuition, a ratio of one adult to twelve children allows the program to pay the staff fees and the fixed expenses with some money left over. Any profit from the preschool or school-age classrooms must be utilized to cover the loss of funds in the younger classrooms.

Since child-care programs rely on the profit from the preschool classrooms, it can be damaging to private programs when a public school program offers free enrollment to preschool students in the community or when families leave the child-care program to enroll in a preschool-to-twelfth-grade private school in the neighborhood. If there are not enough preschool children enrolled to balance the loss of funds in the infant and toddler classrooms, then a program may be forced to drop its infant and toddler care and serve only preschool students. If the enrollment in the preschool classrooms dips significantly, the program may have to close down completely.

STAFFING

Due to low wages, few to no benefits, and a labor-intensive job, many long-term child-care providers have left the field so that they are better able to support their own families. Also, new employees are not entering the field to replace those who are leaving. When child-care programs are not able to fully staff their programs, they must reduce the number of children they can care for, or they may have to close entire classrooms. Some child-care programs have discontinued infant and toddler care completely since those classrooms do not make any profit.

Because private child-care programs offer only entry-level wages, many of the staff members who are working in child care are also entry-level workers with limited training. It can be overwhelming for a new staff member to manage a full classroom of children, especially if some of those children have special needs. To recruit highly trained, experienced early childhood educators, programs will have to find a way to pay their staff members a higher wage without making care so expensive that parents cannot afford it.

OFFERING CHILD CARE FOR FAMILIES WHO WORK NONTRADITIONAL HOURS

The vast majority of child-care programs serve families who work during a typical "office day" and are open from 6 a.m. to 6 p.m.; however, many families work in industries with jobs outside of those hours. Workers at hospitals, factories, restaurants, retail establishments, and other businesses need child care on the weekends or during second- or third-shift schedules. Some of those families may have a family member, a friend, or a trusted babysitter who can help them, but others may have to leave a job or reduce their hours if they cannot find access to safe child care.

Some of these businesses, such as hospitals or large manufacturers, may see a need to add on-site child care for their employees to ensure that they are able to attract the workforce that they need, but only the largest businesses can offer that type of service to their employees. Other families may need to find centers with later hours or family child-care homes that offer overnight care for young children. Family child-care homes can offer more flexible hours for the children enrolled in their programs, but there has been a shortage of family child-care homes in the past five to ten years (Child Care Aware of America, 2020).

INFANT AND TODDLER CARE

Because infant and toddler classrooms have smaller adult-to-child ratios and smaller classroom sizes, there are naturally fewer infant and toddler slots available in all child-care centers. That does not mean that fewer families need infant and toddler care. Some families may have a parent who stays home with a new baby for a year or two before enrolling the child in group child care, but many families do not have that option. Single-parent homes must have infant and toddler care so that the one parent can provide for the family. There are working families with more than one parent in the workforce that need both adults to work to cover expenses such as housing, food, transportation, and college debt. With fewer slots available for infant and toddler care, it can be incredibly challenging for parents to find the child care they need (Mader, 2022).

CHILDREN WITH SPECIAL NEEDS

Finding child care for children with special needs can also be overwhelming. Childcare programs may desperately want to support a child with special needs, but if they are operating with the maximum adult-to-child ratio in each classroom, they may not be able to provide the individualized attention the child requires. This is especially true with entry-level staff members who are struggling to manage a full classroom of children. If a child with a disability exhibits disruptive behaviors or has medical needs that can take a lot of the teacher's time, the teacher may not be able to take care of the class as a whole along with the special needs required for an individual child. In these cases, the teacher may become overwhelmed and wish to quit his position.

Instead of losing the teacher or other children enrolled in the classroom, the director may sit down with the parents of the child with special needs and tell them that the center does not have the resources to support the child. Because private child-care programs do not receive federal funds to support children with disabilities like the public school system does, it may be completely true that the school is not set up to support the child. Unfortunately, the family may hear the same concerns from multiple child-care programs and be turned away again and again. Consider Kerry's story.

> My partner and I have a four-year-old son with autism. Tyler is creative and funny, even though most people don't expect a child with autism to have a sense of humor. He is smart. Many people expect him to be smart like Dustin Hoffman's depiction of Rain Man. Tyler doesn't count toothpicks that have fallen on the floor. He is beginning to read at four years old, mainly because he has memorized so many sight words and all the books that we have read to him over and over again. What he struggles with is meeting new people and encountering new situations. He is dependent on routines, and he struggles with transitions that he doesn't anticipate. When he has a substitute teacher at school, he can really panic. To try and prepare him for the situation, his teacher will call us in advance so that we can let him know what to expect. Sometimes this works, and other times I have to take the day off of work to stay at home with him.
>
> My partner and I both work full-time. Honestly, with Tyler's medical bills, we both need full-time salaries and the best health insurance possible. He has

more doctor visits and therapy appointments each year than many children will have in their lifetime. Because we work full-time, we need full-time child care. That has been one of the biggest challenges that we have faced as the family of a child with a disability. Several child-care programs have told us that they enroll children with disabilities, but after Tyler attends for a few weeks, they begin to change their minds. When he becomes overwhelmed and has a meltdown in the classroom, the teachers don't seem to know what to do. Because teachers have a tendency to change every several months, it can take Tyler another few months to get comfortable with a new teacher. He may not talk to the teachers in his classroom until he has been around them for two to three months. I understand that child-care employees make low wages, so it is hard to keep them for a long time in a low-paying job. The problem is that the staff turnover is so hard on the children, particularly Tyler.

When Tyler is overwhelmed or afraid, he may run and hide. The therapists call that *elopement*, but the child-care program calls that a liability. They are afraid of being sued, and they don't want to put themselves at risk. Tyler can also become very overwhelmed by all the excitement of a classroom filled with preschoolers, and it can cause him to hide or even push the other children away in order for him to get the personal space that he needs to calm down. The teachers and the administrators don't want to be responsible for having to tell another family that their child was hit by a classmate. What usually happens after the first month in a new school is that the administrator will ask my partner and me to come in for a meeting. They never expel him from the program. That would be discrimination against a child with a disability, and no program wants that kind of reputation. Instead, they begin telling us that they don't have the resources in their program for a child like Tyler and that he would be safer somewhere else. Once they start talking about his safety, the burden falls on us. It would obviously sound terrible if we said that we don't care about his safety because we just need child care. Obviously, we want him to be safe, but at this point, we are running out of options.

The public school system in our town has preschool for children like Tyler with diagnosed disabilities, but the preschool class meets only four days a week for three hours a day. Even if we sent him to that program, we would still need a child-care program for the remainder of the school day, and on snow days, school holidays, and summer vacation. The child-care programs in our town don't have teachers trained to work with children with disabilities. Plus, most of the preschool classrooms have up to twenty-four children in each class, and that can be a lot of students to deal with when they don't have issues like Tyler. Add Tyler to the mix, and you know that teachers can get overwhelmed. Ultimately, we need the skilled teachers from the public school system with the hours of operation from a private child-care program. Surely, we aren't the only family that needs this type of care for our child.

CHILD CARE IN RURAL AREAS

Access to child care can be just as complicated in rural areas where there is little to no child care. Small communities are often categorized as child-care deserts, where there is not enough child care for the number of children who need access to care. Rural areas are often more at risk of being child-care deserts because families and homes are often spaced farther apart. Transportation then becomes one of the major obstacles to care. A child-care center needs a larger number of families to enroll in order to pay the fixed expenses and the salaries. If the distance from the center is too far for families to enroll in the program, the child-care center will not be financially successful and will close its doors. Typically, in rural areas, family child-care homes are more successful since they need only a small number of families enrolled to be financially stable.

Although not every challenge for the child-care system may have an immediate answer, several of the challenges could have positive solutions by using a mixed-delivery child-care system. In the next chapter, we'll take a closer look at the mixed-delivery care system and its benefits to private child-care programs, public school preschools, families, and, most importantly, children.

CHAPTER 5

A Possible Solution: Mixed-Delivery Care

The past several years have established that the child-care field is fragile and at risk of collapse. As policy makers have analyzed the field to determine the best way to preserve quality early childhood classrooms, it has also become apparent that there is no single magic solution to fix the problem. Additional funding streams definitely seem to be part of the solution, as well as involving the business community and emphasizing the importance of child care. Staffing the early childhood workforce with qualified teachers is a challenge, and child care will not be able to continue without a skilled workforce. Looking at several of these possible solutions shows that mixing the models of different early childhood systems could potentially make all three systems stronger. The approach of mixing funding and policy of early childhood systems is called a *mixed-delivery systems approach*. Some of the most common examples include the following:

- A Head Start or Early Head Start grantee gives a per-child amount to a private child-care program to serve children who qualify as Head Start or Early Head Start students. The child-care program agrees to follow the Head Start Program Performance Standards (HSPPS) and signs an accountability contract with the Head Start grantee.
- A public school places a classroom inside a private child-care program and provides the teaching staff and support staff, such as a speech pathologist or an occupational therapist, with professional-development training. The public school district may not provide a per-child amount to the center, but the school

may receive a general stipend for resources, playground equipment, consumable supplies, or teacher training.
- A Head Start program operates in a public school with teachers from both the public school and the Head Start grantee. The classroom uses both state and federal funding, and it also adheres to school-district and federal HSPPS.
- A public school district partners with a private child-care program. The public school system pays a per-child amount to the child-care program to enroll children who qualify for the state-funded public school classroom.
- An Early Head Start program partners with a family child-care home. The family child-care home program receives a per-child amount of federal funding if the program meets the Early Head Start Program Standards.

Different communities may find unique ways to blend state-funded preschool, Head Start, and private child-care programs based on the needs of the community and the agencies' abilities to meet all the different program requirements (Griffey, 2016). Also, the community may be limited to what programs can blend together if it is a child-care desert and there is no private child care in the area.

HOW DOES MIXED DELIVERY WORK?

The concept of mixed-delivery early childhood education is to make sure that the needs of the families are met by blending two of the different models together. For example, many public school and Head Start programs are only half-day programs, but most working families need child care that lasts at least eight to eight and a half hours per day in order to make sure that the child's parent or guardian can work a full day. Each program has its own benefits, whether that is funding, family supports, or curriculum, so the community needs to look at the resources needed to decide how best to pair the available programs. A well-blended program will include:

- consistent, year-round care;
- equitable access to high-quality care and education;
- well-trained and experienced teachers;
- affordability for families;
- family choice; and
- different cultural models, including neighborhood care, faith-based care, dual-language care, community-center care, center-based care, and in-home care.

It can be much easier for state-funded preschool and Head Start to partner together, since the government funding streams require a higher level of teacher education and quality initiatives. Because child-care programs are independent small businesses, the level of quality can vary greatly depending on the vision and mission of the child-care programs' leadership teams. If a child-care program already operates at a high level of quality and hires experienced staff, then the program may need very few modifications to partner with a publicly funded program; however, a child-care program that meets only its state's minimum licensing requirements may have to initiate dramatic policy changes to meet the requirements of a publicly funded contract.

Regardless of the programs' funding streams or hours of operation, all quality early care and education programs must be led by child-development principles. Families need the security of knowing that their children will be safe and cared for in any early education program across the mixed-delivery system. Teachers should establish consistent routines (not necessarily timed schedules, but the order of classroom activities) in each classroom. The adults who teach and guide the children in the classroom should have quality interactions with each child during the school day, as well as a knowledge of child development, experience working with children in a group setting, and a history of establishing positive relationships with the children's families. Partnerships with families should be at the center of the program's mission since the family members are truly the experts on their children.

HOW CAN MIXED DELIVERY BENEFIT FAMILIES?

Families receive multiple benefits when they can participate in mixed-delivery programs, including accessing child care when they need it and having greater choice when selecting child-care programs.

FLEXIBLE HOURS

One of the biggest benefits of mixed-delivery programs for families is having care and education for their children throughout working hours. Many government-funded early childhood programs operate for only a half-day per child. (Teachers may teach for a full day, but they may have one class of students in the morning and a second group of students in the afternoon.) A half-day schedule may not be a problem if one parent has an extremely flexible work schedule or is not employed outside the home. However, in many households, every adult living in the home must have a job to best support the family. As a result, parents cannot leave work in the middle of the day to transport their children from one type of care to a second type of care.

The child may also have a difficult time with this type of large transition, making it even more complicated for the family member to leave the child at a second early education program and return to work on time. Families need an early care setting that will be open the full length of the workday. When a government-funded program partners with a private child-care program, families have the opportunity to select one classroom for their children for the full school day without having to worry about whether or not the child-care hours will cover the parents' workday.

The mixed-delivery system can also offer the full-year care that families require. Government-funded child-care programs not only close for federal holidays but may also close for winter break, spring break, summer vacation, and brief holidays such as President's Day or Election Day. This break in care can be extremely hard for families who work in industries that do not often close, such as grocery stores, hospitals, restaurants, and other service industries. The summer vacation from school can also be inconvenient for all families, unless someone in the home is a teacher and is also off for the break. Private child care offers that consistent year-round care, and when children are already enrolled in the program through the mixed-delivery system, they typically have the first opportunity to attend the child-care program on those scheduled and unscheduled breaks from school.

Parents who work nontraditional hours have an even more challenging time finding consistent care for their children. This typically includes parents who work second or third shift or on weekends. Not only are government-funded early education programs closed during these hours, but most child-care centers are also closed during this time. This is only one of the reasons why it is so important to include family child-care homes in the mixed-delivery model of early education (Lieberman, 2021). Family child-care homes have more flexibility to establish their hours around the needs of the community and the families they serve. Unlike a center opening on nights and weekends that would require multiple staff members to agree to work nontraditional hours, family child-care providers can set up their own schedule to support the parents who enroll in the program. Consider Rina's story.

> I was so grateful when I finally got a job offer from the car manufacturing company in our town. For years, I have heard about the amazing health insurance and retirement plan that they offer their employees. I didn't realize that there were other benefits such as a free gym membership and an on-site doctor's clinic at the plant. The company even offers paid leave for a birth in the family or an adoption. When I met with the human resources manager, she shared my starting hourly salary, and I was so happy. I immediately accepted the position. Then, she told me to slow down and listen to the rest of the offer. All new staff members must start by working on second or

third shift. I was not expecting that. I am a single parent of a three-year-old daughter, and I cannot leave her alone at night. Her current child-care program is open from 6 a.m. to 6 p.m., which works well for a day job. I have never seen a child-care program that is open at night, and I don't have any family members who could watch Mae at night.

A friend told me that she knew of a woman in our neighborhood who had a preschool in the basement of her home, and she had about five children that she took care of each day. My friend had talked about how much she loved sending her child there because, if she had to work overtime or on the weekend, she could tell the child-care teacher what her hours were and she would work with her. Her daughter had stayed at her house until 11 p.m. one night, and the teacher just put her to sleep on her nap mat until her mom got there. I thought it was fabulous that she also watched her daughter on a Saturday, because none of the child-care centers are open then. I have just never seen programs like this advertised before. I don't want to turn down a job like this, because it could be such a great opportunity for our little family. I think I just need to find a way to find one of those preschool homes for my daughter.

GREATER CHOICE WHEN SELECTING CHILD-CARE PROGRAMS

Mixed-delivery early education systems also allow families to have more choice about their children's early education needs. Hours and location are two things that families can choose when selecting a child-care program that partners with a government-funded program. Families also have the opportunity to consider the primary language spoken in the child-care program, the cultural background, whether it is a center or a home, as well as other defining characteristics of the child-care setting. In a preschool classroom that is completely housed within the public school system, a family can register for preschool if they fit the district's criteria. Then, the family is typically assigned to the preschool classroom that is closest to the family's residence.

The family does not get to meet the teacher in advance and decide if the atmosphere is a good fit for the child. This is obviously like the operational method of the elementary and secondary school system, but leaving a toddler or a preschool age student with a stranger for the first time is a very different experience for parents. The child may not yet be able to tell family members if there is a problem at school. It may be the first time that the child has ever been left with someone outside of the family. It is important to make this first care and education experience as positive and comfortable as possible for the children and the families. Allowing families to have as much choice as possible can establish trust and assurance for future years.

HOW CAN MIXED DELIVERY BENEFIT PUBLIC SCHOOLS?

The mixed-delivery approach to early childhood care helps public schools in a variety of ways, including by reducing the school's expenditures and identifying children with potential disabilities before they enter kindergarten.

FEWER EXPENDITURES

Policy makers may wonder about the effect of sharing public school system funds with private businesses and how that would affect the state system. This is not a reflection on the type of care and education that the public school system offers to young children; instead, it is a discussion about the realistic capacity that the school system has to offer. When a public school system opens enrollment to more and more preschool-aged children within its district, it must also provide additional classrooms to educate those children as well as professionally trained teachers who will work in each classroom.

When elementary schools are built, preschool classrooms are typically an afterthought. There may be one or two classrooms in the building that are designated for preschool students. Sometimes, those classrooms are modified for other students when kindergarten and primary enrollment increases and more space is needed. Some districts may even have to move their preschool classrooms to portable classroom units located behind the school until building expansions can be made. Building new classrooms, and even new schools, is a huge capital investment, but it is unnecessary if the school district has strong partnerships with high-quality child-care programs in the area.

Instead of spending millions of dollars on new buildings, the school district can contract with high-quality child-care programs to reserve a certain number of slots at each program for children who qualify for public-school preschool by the district's enrollment standards. Those programs already have preschool-sized classrooms with trained teachers. The school district can choose how to assign families to the different child-care programs. In many cases, a child has already attended an infant and toddler program at one child-care center or family child-care home, and the family will want the child to continue there. The child-care program can talk to the family about their eligibility for the public school partnership slot and help them file the necessary documents to enroll.

If a child comes to the school district and is not currently enrolled in a child-care program that participates in a mixed-delivery system, then the school can offer the child a spot in a public school classroom or show the family the options for a mixed-delivery child-care program, allowing them to see what setting would be best for the child and the family. With the understanding that the care and education components are equitable at all options, families do not have to base their decision solely on the program's reputation. Instead, they can choose a program that can support the whole family while helping prepare the child for kindergarten.

PROMOTING EQUITY AND INCLUSION

In the field of early childhood education, the programs that provide the highest-quality care typically cost the most money to operate. This is because many of the signs of a high-quality program—educated and well-trained teachers, lower staff-to-child ratios, smaller class sizes—require more money to achieve. By those standards, whichever families can pay the most for child care can obtain high-quality care for their children. When the federal and/or state government subsidizes the cost for the families, as in state-funded preschool or Head Start, then families with lower incomes can still access high-quality early education for their children.

A variety of families have access to high-quality, half-day services through government-funded programs, but that still means that full-day, quality early childhood education may be out of reach for some families.

In a mixed-delivery system, equitable access is open to all families regardless of what part of the community they live in, the family's income level, the child's ability level, or the ethnic and racial background of the family (Huey, 2021). It also means if a family were to move from one program to another due to a change in residence or a need for different hours of operation, the quality of the program and the available resources should be equitable. To make sure that all children are prepared to enter kindergarten, the community must develop an equitable system that allows all children to be as successful as possible.

EARLY IDENTIFICATION OF CHILDREN WITH DISABILITIES

Partnering with child-care programs and Head Start programs also helps the public school district identify as many children as possible with potential disabilities before the children begin kindergarten. Given the length of the identification and evaluation process, a new kindergarten student may not be able to obtain special education services until the middle of the second semester of the school year. If an increase of preschool enrollment due to partnership locations allows more children to be served in preschool, then more children will have the opportunity to enter kindergarten with their special education services in place, or they will have already been receiving special education resources during preschool to make kindergarten an even more successful school year.

HOW DOES MIXED DELIVERY BENEFIT PRIVATE CHILD-CARE PROGRAMS?

Mixed-delivery care benefits private child-care programs by providing them with a stable revenue stream, support for children with special needs, and a more diverse population of children and staff. By stabilizing the child-care market as a whole, the mixed-delivery care approach can be the lifeline that the private child-care industry so desperately needs.

STABLE REVENUE STREAMS

Typical private child-care programs receive most of their income from tuition paid by families. Some of those families may use a government subsidy, but it is still a payment equivalent to the tuition. The tuition amount is typically set by what parents can afford, not what quality child care actually costs. When a private child-care program partners with Head Start and Early Head Start or the local school district, there is usually a contractual stipend that the government-funded organization will offer the program over the course of the year to care for a certain number of children. Mixed-delivery child-care programs have the opportunity to receive multiple streams of funding, which can then be used to help stabilize the financial structure of the program.

SERVICES TO SUPPORT CHILDREN WITH SPECIAL NEEDS

A government-funded agency, such as the school system or a Head Start–funded organization, may also provide services that a private child-care program would not have had access to, such as special education services. In that case, a school district will most likely ask the staff it already employs to visit the child-care program. The children will get the benefit of working with trained therapists, and the program's teachers will get training from these professionals to better support children in the classroom. Sometimes, those extra resources and support can be enough to help an early childhood educator feel more confident in the classroom and more willing to continue working in a challenging classroom environment.

A MORE DIVERSE COMMUNITY

Because the cost of child care often determines where a family can or cannot enroll their children, a mixed-delivery child-care partnership can allow a private child-care program to serve a more diverse group of students and work with a variety of families. Tuition requirements often make it too challenging for some child-care programs to serve all the families in their community. They may have to turn away children and families they want to serve simply because the families cannot find an additional forty dollars a week to pay for tuition. Mixed-delivery partnerships can allow child-care programs the opportunity to support a variety of the families in the community because the school district or the Head Start grantee is subsidizing the cost of tuition for the families.

STABILIZATION OF THE CHILD-CARE MARKET

The greatest benefit of the mixed-delivery partnership system for child care is probably the stabilization of the child-care market. When some states have significantly expanded access to public-school preschool or even adopted universal pre-K strictly through the public school system, it has caused a collapse of the child-care system (Policy Equity Group, 2023). Child-care programs count on having successful enrollment in their preschool classrooms to offset the financial loss generated by infant and toddler classrooms. Infant tuition is typically more expensive than preschool tuition, but the financial difference is not enough to cover the cost of the smaller adult-to-infant or -toddler ratio. When centers lose all, or a significant number of, the preschool students to public-school preschool, they do not have any additional funds to cover the loss in the infant and toddler classrooms. This type of financial loss makes it impossible for the program to remain open.

When a community has universal pre-K but no (or limited) infant and toddler care, the families in the community still suffer an overall loss. Many families may have to completely leave the workforce for several years until the youngest child is old enough for preschool. Still, appropriate child-care options for preschool students may not be available during the public school breaks. That lack may prevent family members from consistently holding jobs.

Of course, the workforce will suffer with large numbers of families leaving their jobs, but it is also important to remember the impact that a loss of child care can have on the family. Losing an income (or even a partial income) can make the family financially unstable. Families may need additional government supports to maintain stable nutrition, medical care, or housing. Families may also be affected by increased stress in the family during these unstable times. Overall, a stable child-care market is a huge benefit for the centers, the families, and the economy as a whole.

WHAT ARE THE BENEFITS FOR CHILDREN?

Just as families, private child-care programs, and public school districts benefit from mixed-delivery early education systems, young children also benefit from this complex system. A mixed-delivery care system offers children a consistent environment and specialized care as needed.

A CONSISTENT ENVIRONMENT

One of the best benefits for young children is the consistent environment that is provided through mixed delivery. Children can be enrolled in the same program all day, all year, from birth until they start kindergarten, and with siblings and trusted teachers.

When the public school system, the Head Start grantee, and the private child-care programs all operate independently, then children may attend several child-care programs per day and during the course of the week. Parents may have to take infants and toddlers to one program and drop off preschoolers at another, and possibly at programs that have different hours of operation and are on different sides of town. Families may have to begin looking for summer child care beginning in January to ensure that they do not have to reduce their work hours over the summer or take leave from work. Collaboration through mixed delivery reduces the stress on the whole family and allows children to know what to expect by arriving in the same classroom environment or in-home program each day.

SPECIALIZED CARE IF NEEDED

It is also beneficial for children with disabilities or special health-care needs or those who have experienced trauma to get specialized care, regardless of what building they attend each day. Additional teacher training on health-care needs, disabilities, and trauma-informed care are frequently provided by Head Start grantees and the public school system, when some child-care programs may not have the funding to get research-based training on such specific topics. It is a true asset for families and children when the child receives early intervention in the classroom from a trained professional, and it is even a greater benefit when the teacher can continue to implement those therapy strategies through the rest of the school day.

Children can start off having positive feelings about school and about special education, instead of dreading going to school each day knowing that they will struggle or get in trouble. Early intervention from a speech pathologist or other specialist also gives the student the opportunity to begin meeting his or her developmental milestones sooner than anticipated. A child receiving early intervention in the toddler or preschool classroom may not even need those same supports later in elementary school, and that means more time when the student will not struggle with schoolwork.

Mixed-delivery care can be a viable solution to the current child-care crisis. In the next chapter, we will look at a type of mixed-delivery care—public-private partnerships—to see how overlapping the benefits of the Head Start system or the state-funded preschool system can have positive benefits for struggling child-care programs.

CHAPTER 6

Public-Private Partnerships

Public-private partnerships are a special type of mixed-delivery education in which a private child-care program partners with either a state-funded preschool or Head Start/Early Head Start. When a private child-care program teams with a government-funded early education program, the private program may have to raise its quality standards, but the partnership also increases the program's financial stability. For example, if a public school district provides a private program with a per-child amount of funding that is designated for public school students, then the child-care program will receive:

- a consistent funding source for the length of the school year;
- an attractive teaching environment for staff with higher levels of experience and education;
- special-education resources, such as visits from speech pathologists or physical therapists; and
- professional development training offered through the public school system.

Also, the child-care program still has the opportunity to receive child-care subsidy for children who meet the state's income eligibility requirements, so this additional funding can assist with covering the cost of care on days when the school system is not open, such as holidays or summer break.

One of the greatest benefits of these partnerships is enhanced special education supports. Child-care programs do not receive special education supports as the public school systems do. If a child with a disability is enrolled in a private child-care program, there is a strong possibility that staff members do not know how to best support the child in being successful. This lack of resources often leads to children being suspended or expelled from private child-care facilities, and suspension and expulsion is a growing problem in private child-care programs. A research study by Yale University Child Development Center showed that children between the ages of birth and five years are much more likely to be expelled from an education program than children who attend an elementary or secondary school (Meek and Gilliam, 2016).

Child-care administrators may have to have uncomfortable conversations with families advising them to look elsewhere for child care. This is not due to discrimination against children with disabilities; instead, it is because the programs do not have the training or resources to support the children. When a public-private partnership occurs as a part of a mixed-delivery early childhood system, there is a more even distribution of limited resources so that all families can receive support.

HEAD START AND PRIVATE CHILD CARE'S ESTABLISHED ALLIANCE

Many Head Start programs are practiced at operating a partnership with private child-care programs. In many states, a Head Start program that is not part of the public school system will also become a licensed child-care program to participate in the state's subsidized child-care system. This means that Head Start programs must understand and meet the child-care licensing requirements as well as the Head Start Program Performance Standards (HSPPS). The child-care licensing requirements are usually minimal in comparison to the HSPPS, so other than keeping state documentation and undergoing annual inspections by the state, the Head Start program does not usually take on any additional responsibilities. On the other hand, a typical private child-care program would have to make significant changes to its setup and administration to meet the requirements of all Head Start programs.

Despite the challenge, Head Start grantees have been utilizing private child-care partnerships for quite some time. For example, a Head Start grantee may receive three hundred Head Start slots for the community it serves, but it can house only two hundred fifty of those slots in its own facilities. The grantee would then partner with local child-care programs to accommodate the other fifty slots. Typically, the grantee would form relationships with child-care programs in the communities where potential Head Start families live, reducing potential transportation issues and allowing families to feel a greater sense of trust if they already know the community and the child-care program. The grantee would show the child-care program the benefits of being a Head Start partner and would discuss the requirements for the program's participation.

If both organizations can agree to the partnership, then the grantee designates a certain number of Head Start slots for that child-care program, and the child-care director finds children for those slots who are eligible by the Head Start criteria. The family of the Head Start child would then need to fill out the Head Start enrollment paperwork, but the family members (the child and the adults) then have access to many more resources; additionally, Head Start covers the child's full cost of tuition. The child may already be enrolled in the private child-care program, but participation in Head Start would offer the child more benefits, and the family would have access to Head Start's wrap-around supports. If the child-care program has empty slots, then the grantee's family service workers could potentially direct families who qualify for Head Start services to the center.

EARLY HEAD START-CHILD CARE PARTNERSHIP

In his 2013 State of the Union address to the nation, President Barack Obama talked about the benefit of Head Start programs and the need to offer more spots for infants and toddlers (First Five Years Fund, 2022). In 2014, the Office of Head Start started a program called Early Head Start Partnerships, and it received a distinct line of funding, along with its own grant application process. The Department of Health and Human Services awards money to the Early Head Start-Child Care Partnership (EHS-CCP) grantee to work with local child-care programs, including both centers and family child-care homes. To qualify as a partner, the child-care center or family child-care home must serve low-income families who would meet the Early Head Start eligibility requirements, and they must agree to follow Head Start Program Standards. The Early Head Start grantees also agree to assist the partners in meeting the requirements by providing access to resources and wrap-around services such as screenings, health and nutrition needs, developmental supports, and teacher training.

The Early Head Start grantee will award funding to the partnering child-care program based on the number of enrollment slots that the child-care program accepts. These funds can be used by the child-care provider to increase teacher compensation, reduce classroom sizes, lower the adult-to-child ratio in the classrooms, provide supplies, pay for equipment and facility repairs, or provide teacher training (First Five Years Fund, 2022). The grantee also receives separate funds designated for offering technical assistance to the partnership sites and assuring fidelity to the Head Start Performance Standards. Along with the stipend from the Early Head Start grantee, child-care programs are encouraged to use state child-care subsidies provided through the Child Care and Development Block Grant. With a combination of Early Head Start funding and child-care funding, the center or family child-care home has the best opportunity to offer the children and families a high-quality learning environment.

Although the program began only in 2014, by 2017 there were 275 Early Head Start grantees that were partnering with 1,400 child-care centers and 1,000 family child-care homes (First Five Years Fund, 2022). This allowed more than 32,000 children to be served through the new Early Head Start Partnership program. And, even though they were not enrolled in Early Head Start, an additional 7,800 children benefitted from being in smaller classrooms with reduced adult-to-child ratios and highly trained teachers. By the 2020 federal fiscal year, the United States was investing $905 million in Early Head Start Partnership grants (First Five Years Fund, 2022).

The new infusion of funding into private child care was definitely benefitting all children who were enrolled. More than half of Early Head Start Partnerships were using some of their additional funds to make sure that all children enrolled in their programs were offered screenings for vision, hearing, dental, speech, development, nutrition, and lead exposure (Smith, Campbell, Tracey, and Pluta-Ehlers, 2019). More than one-third of the partnership sites were using additional funding to provide mental-health screenings, health and mental-health services, or speech and physical therapy. The breakdown of some other funds includes the following:

- Eighty-five percent of centers and 86 percent of family child-care homes offered coaching, mentoring, and technical assistance training to their staff members.
- Seventy-three percent of centers and 75 percent of family child-care homes purchased age-appropriate furniture.
- Fifty-nine percent of centers and 50 percent of family child-care homes purchased playground equipment or updated their playgrounds.
- Seventy-four percent of centers and 66 percent of family child-care homes purchased a research-based curriculum.
- Sixty-nine percent of centers and 70 percent of family child-care homes purchased new books.

(Smith, Campbell, Tracey, and Pluta-Ehlers, 2019)

Again, these additions benefit the Early Head Start students, but every student enrolled in the program benefits as well. If one classroom has four Early Head Start students enrolled in it, then the other four children attending receive these same benefits and have the opportunity for a higher-quality early childhood education.

QUALITY COMPONENTS

When a grantee looks for child-care programs to partner with for an EHS-CCP grant, they can consider centers, family child-care homes, or a combination of the two. There are slightly different requirements for centers compared to family homes, so the grantee must outline those requirements from the beginning of the partnership.

Adult-to-Child Ratio

Early Head Start center-based care must have one teacher for every four infants and/or toddlers, and it must maintain a maximum classroom size of eight children (Office of Head Start, 2022). In a family child-care home, one provider can care for a maximum of six children with no more than two children under the age of two. If the family child-care home has a provider and an assistant, the maximum group size can be twelve children, but there can be no more than four infants and/or toddlers. Only two of those children can be under the age of eighteen months.

Classroom and Staffing Requirements

Early Head Start programs have established quality markers, indicated in the HSPPS, that must be implemented in each EHS classroom to meet minimum requirements. For example, to establish continuity for the children being cared for, Early Head Start requires that each child have a primary caregiver in the classroom, and each classroom should maintain year-round services to establish consistent routines (Office of Head Start, 2022). To promote healthy child development in all Early Head Start classrooms, the performance standards require an evidence-based curriculum with aligned teaching practices, ongoing child assessment at multiple points during the year, individualized lessons based on the abilities of the child, and continuous program improvement measures to make sure that the education program is being implemented in the most successful manner possible.

Education requirements are different for centers and family child-care homes. An Early Head Start teacher in a child-care program must have a Child Development Associate's (CDA) certificate with a focus on infants and toddlers (Office of Head Start, 2022). Early Head Start teachers in a family child-care home must be enrolled in a program to receive a CDA certificate, and the certificate must be completed within eighteen months.

Physical and Mental Health Services

Promoting physical and mental health are also key characteristics of the HSPPS. Early Head Start classrooms are responsible for conducting a variety of health screenings throughout the year and referring children for additional supports if needed (Office of Head Start, 2022). These screenings include vision, dental, hearing, and other indicators. A partnership site may not have access to these types of screening tools, but this is a perfect example of how the grantee can support a partner program. The grantee may simply select several days when staff members or contract professionals visit each partnership classroom to conduct the necessary screenings. Then, if any child scores low on the screening and indicates that a follow-up appointment is needed, the grantee can help arrange that visit.

In the event that the family is not able to help a child obtain medical or dental services, particularly after a referral has been made, the Early Head Start grantee is responsible for helping the child get the assistance needed. The grantee may help the partner program take the child to a well-child exam, to get immunizations at the health department, or to the dentist to get a filling for a cavity (Office of Head Start, 2022). The Early Head Start classroom also assists with the child's nutrition. All Early Head Start programs must participate in the Child and Adult Care Food Program (CACFP), which establishes nutrition guidelines for food served in child-care programs and also reimburses child-care programs for money spent on healthy foods based on the income-level and the number of children enrolled. If an infant is not yet eating solid food, then the Early Head Start classroom can provide formula for the child while at the program.

Healthy and Safe Classroom Environments

All Early Head Start classrooms must maintain a healthy and safe classroom environment (Office of Head Start, 2022). For an infant, this may start with implementing safe sleep practices by placing the infant on his back to sleep with nothing else in the crib. It may also be essential for the Early Head Start teaching staff to offer guidance to parents on how to implement safe sleep practices at home. Once the infant or toddler is outside of the crib and exploring the classroom environment, many other safety policies must be in place.

All classrooms must have a procedure for cleaning and sanitizing to minimize the germs in the classroom. There must be safe eating guidelines such as not propping a bottle in a child's mouth while she is drinking and having children who are able sit at a table when eating any type of food. Most health and safety requirements will also be outlined in the state's child-care licensing regulations, so partnering child-care programs should already be aware of how to run a healthy and safe classroom. However, some additional requirements, such as safe sleep policies, may be new to the classroom staff.

Family and Community Partnerships

Head Start and Early Head Start programs establish a greater focus on family and community partnerships than most typical child-care programs do, so it may initially feel unfamiliar for a child-care program to implement some of the program standards regarding families. All high-quality early childhood education programs attempt to establish a strong communication system with families. Beyond daily communication, Early Head Start programs also attempt to offer a great deal of family education (Office of Head Start, 2022). This may include regular family education meetings, information sent home by handout or email, or even one-on-one education in the classroom setting. Parents also can be a part of parent and community councils for their local Head Start communities. This opportunity gives parents a voice on staffing, program activities, and community engagement opportunities.

Early Head Start classrooms also provide families with two home visits per year (Office of Head Start, 2022). This can be a new experience for many child-care providers, and the grantee is able to offer training to the child-care program teachers on how to conduct a home visit, what type of information to cover, and how to develop deeper parent-teacher relationships. As the family members begin to feel more comfortable with the teachers, they may feel safe sharing information about what types of resources they need. This is another area in which Head Start grantees excel. Family service workers can help families connect to organizations that can provide food, help with paying utilities, or support filling out government subsidy applications.

BENEFITS OF THE EARLY HEAD START-CHILD CARE PARTNERSHIP

Although a partnership can pose some challenges on both sides of the agreement, the Early Head Start partnerships with child-care programs ultimately provide benefits for everyone involved.

PROVIDING CARE OUTSIDE TYPICAL WORK HOURS

One of the greatest benefits of the partnership program for working families is that private child-care programs offer more hours of care. Most private child-care programs are open for ten- to twelve-hour days, so the Early Head Start Partnership participants benefit from the full-day, full-year access of a community child-care program. Of course, children enrolled in an Early Head Start classroom within a grantee's program or within a child-care partnership will receive a free, high-quality early childhood education with wrap-around benefits for the child's wellness and parent engagement. The extended hours of care at the child-care program can benefit many families trying to maintain a work schedule.

Giving Families More Choices in Program Selection

Parents have more choices about which program they would like their children to attend. This means that a family may have the option to choose a faith-based child-care program, a program where the employees speak the same language as the family, or a smaller family child-care home where different-aged siblings can be together. The goal is to make sure that the program can meet the needs of the child and the family it is serving, whether that means location, hours of operation, or cultural diversity.

IMPROVING THE WORK ENVIRONMENT FOR STAFF

Teachers in the child-care sites can also experience greater benefits from the partnership. First, having a smaller class and lower adult-to-child ratio can significantly decrease a teacher's stress level. It is better for each teacher to be responsible for caring for four infants or toddlers than for five or six. Teachers also benefit from increased professional development. Additional job training can help teachers feel more prepared and confident in the classroom.

Beyond professional development training, teachers in an Early Head Start classroom have the additional opportunity to pursue a CDA certificate if they have not already obtained one. This certificate is not only an investment of time, but it can cost the teacher a large amount of money that the Early Head Start grantee is able to cover. A teacher with additional credentials and more training is valued more highly in the workforce, so the program is not only helping the teacher learn but also making him more marketable. With that in mind, the Early Head Start partnership also provides the funding for the teachers to have a higher salary. Although most teachers do not pursue a career in early childhood education due to salary, they still need to make enough money to support their own families. This infusion of funding in the child-care program can help maintain higher salaries and can also show the teaching staff a higher level of respect for the job that they do.

The administrators of the private child-care programs benefit from the partnerships as well. First, the child-care centers and family child-care homes are not competing against the Early Head Start classrooms. Instead of losing paying families who transfer to Early Head Start to enjoy a free early childhood education, child-care programs can retain their enrollment and receive the full amount of funding for each student from the Early Head Start grantee. This allows the child-care program to keep full enrollment and potentially be financially stable.

IMPROVED OVERALL QUALITY FOR BOTH PARTNERS

The other major benefit for private child-care programs is that the Early Head Start grantee allows the child-care program to increase its overall quality with:

- reduced adult-to-child ratios and more attention for each child;
- improved professional development for all teaching staff;
- on-site technical assistance and staff mentoring;
- high-quality curriculum; and
- funds to provide vision, hearing, dental, speech, and developmental screenings to all the children enrolled in the child-care program.

These tools not only benefit the children enrolled, but they also offer several benefits to the child-care program. First, with lower child-teacher ratios and more training, teachers are likely to experience less stress in their workplace. This is one way to reduce staff turnover. Second, since many of these benefits affect the tuition-paying students as well as the Early Head Start students, they become a marketing tool for child-care programs to display when recruiting and enrolling new families. Based on high tuition rates, families are looking for the highest quality care for the lowest cost. If potential tuition-paying families see all the resources that the child-care program has available, they are more likely to enroll their children in the child-care program. Also, the funding provided by the Early Head Start grantee can allow partnering child-care programs to provide competitive salaries within the early childhood education field. In the current workforce shortage, a slightly higher salary can be the difference between finding new staff members and having no one apply for an available position.

Finally, the Early Head Start grantee benefits from the partnership as well. It is hard for any grantee to acquire all the available facility space in the area to serve the number of children in the grant. Partnering with high-quality child-care programs can save a great deal of money on the capital expenses it would cost to build new facilities. Also, because the child-care programs already have many staff members in place, the grantee may not have to find new staff members to care for every child who can enroll with the available grant slots.

CHALLENGES FOR EARLY HEAD START-CHILD CARE PARTNERSHIPS

Even with all the benefits of the partnership program, some challenges still must be overcome. One of the first, especially for new grantees, is to find a way to coordinate enrollment and waiting lists among all the programs that the grantee supervises (Reed et al., 2019). In an attempt to coordinate the enrollment process, many programs have one initial application for all the prospective Early Head Start families. Of course, parents may not understand that Early Head Start is working within a private child-care program. Some parents hear word-of-mouth conversation that a certain child-care program has free enrollment for low-income families, and they go directly to apply at the child-care program without understanding that Early Head Start is involved. That family could be on the waitlist for a tuition-paying spot without knowing that there is an Early Head Start slot available at the same location. It is essential for the grantee to determine the best way to communicate with all of the private child-care partners and to use consumer-education materials to reach potential families in the area.

ADAPTING TO NEW STANDARDS

It can also be quite a challenge when a state's child-care licensing requirements are significantly different than the Head Start Performance Standards (Reed et al., 2019). A new child-care partner may automatically default to following some of the state's licensing regulations without taking the time to learn all the expectations of the Early Head Start program. It may require the grantee's technical assistance coaches to invest more time with the partner at the beginning of their relationship to help the organization understand the expectations. If the state has much lower licensing standards, the child-care program may be resistant to transitioning to higher quality standards, such as smaller classroom sizes, that will obviously cost the program more money. The program may be able to afford these increases in quality with the new funding, but operating at the minimum requirements to save money may be an old habit. This transition will take time and a lot of staff training.

UNDERSTANDING FUNDING STREAMS

When a child-care program receives multiple streams of funding, such as Early Head Start funds, child-care subsidy funds, and tuition, it is critical for the program to learn the requirements placed on each funding stream (Reed et al., 2019). This is the same for the grantee at the larger level. Federal funds, whether from Head Start or from the Child Care and Development Block Grant, have certain requirements attached to them. For the purposes of audits and accountability, the administrator will need to document which funding stream paid for which expenses. Any tuition or private donations have a lot more flexibility on how they can be used, but state and federal funding streams will need official documentation. Whoever does the documentation and the financial planning will need to understand the requirements for each set of funding.

GAINING ADMINISTRATIVE, STAFF, AND COMMUNITY BUY-IN

Finally, it is also important for these partnerships to have buy-in from the top administrators all the way down to the teachers in the classroom setting (Reed et al., 2019). If the board of directors for the grantee wrote the grant to receive funding for Early Head Start partnerships, but the Head Start director does not see the purpose, that doubt will trickle down through the entire education program. Superintendents, school boards, child-care program owners, and all management must understand and express the need for these partnerships within the community. When the vision leaders for an organization have faith in this type of program, then middle management and teaching staff will begin to see the support that the program has and will step up to the task. If there are doubts and complaints about the project, then the classroom teachers who are on the front lines of these partnerships will not want to invest the time and effort into administrative changes that they do not believe will last for long.

Despite some administrative and staffing challenges, the Early Head Start program has proven to be effective since its inception in 2014, and its enrollment has continued to grow. The largest request for policy makers is for continued increases to funding so that Early Head Start can expand to the same capacity as the Head Start preschool program. Even when an area has enough preschool capacity to meet the needs of the families who live there, it can still be a child-care desert for infant and toddler care. Partnerships with Early Head Start are one solution to the child-care crisis, and the federal government can assist by providing that increased enrollment.

PRIVATE CHILD CARE AND STATE-FUNDED PRESCHOOL PARTNERSHIPS

State-funded preschool programs in each state vary wildly depending on the state's funding mechanisms and the eligibility criteria that have been established for enrollment. A partnership between a private child-care program and a state-funded preschool is going to look different in each state because the objective of each program is different. The part of the partnership that is the same across each state is that it is a Public-Private Partnership (PPP). PPPs are becoming more and more common, and they are used across sectors throughout the United States.

In recent years there has been a significant increase in enrollment in early childhood education programs, but the growing enrollment is also showing an increasing number of inequities (Gustafsson-Wright, Smith, and Gardiner, 2017). Children from families with higher incomes are accessing high-quality private early childhood programs, while children from low-income families are able to access publicly funded early childhood education that may offer only half-day services or be limited to a few days a week. The same discrepancies are happening to children with disabilities and children in hard-to-reach neighborhoods. The families are not getting all the services that they need.

Some of these complications are occurring because the government capacity is very limited (Gustafsson-Wright, Smith, and Gardiner, 2017). If a state-funded preschool classroom must serve forty-two children, then it needs to have a morning session and an afternoon session to provide the same service to all the children who need support. Without a larger amount of physical building space, teaching staff, and special-education support, there is no way to offer all the participating children full-day services for five days per week. Therefore, children from more affluent families are receiving full-day early childhood education for five days per week, and children with fewer resources are receiving less than half of that amount of support. That puts children from low-income families at a definite disadvantage before the children even start kindergarten.

From a different perspective, private child-care programs have much more flexibility on how to provide services to their clients, especially when it comes to avoiding bureaucracy (Gustafsson-Wright, Smith, and Gardiner, 2017). A private child-care program is likely to be more worried about meeting the needs of the families of the children it cares for than providing care to every child who applies to the program. This means a private program may offer twelve hours of care per day for five days per week. Outside of hours of operation, a private program can look at different ways to be innovative to suit the clients' needs.

If families want teachers who speak the home languages of the children enrolled, the private programs can look to hire staff with that skill set. If many of the families in town work for a manufacturer or hospital that has second- and third-shift employees, the child-care program can find a way to offer evening care to meet the needs of those families. The private program may have to apply for a permit from the state to open during non-traditional hours; however, it doesn't have to worry about whether or not every other program in the state offers nighttime child care and how fair it is for only one program to do that.

With these identified differences between access to public and private child care, it may be possible to close the gap of services between public and private organizations by allowing for PPPs.

THE BASICS OF PUBLIC-PRIVATE PARTNERSHIPS

The basic function of a PPP is to leverage government funding and resources to bring services to the public that are evaluated by the private market (Gustafsson-Wright, Smith, and Gardiner, 2017). In child care, those services may be hours of operation, location, cultural teachings, faith-based services, or curriculum-based education systems. The three main goals of the PPPs in the early childhood education community include improving quality, enhancing equity, and targeting poor or marginalized communities (Gustafsson-Wright, Smith, and Gardiner, 2017).

In other sectors, improving quality through a PPP may mean that the private sector has the higher quality, and the partnership challenges the government agency to increase its quality as well. In the early childhood education sector, both the public sector and the private sector have areas to improve upon. The private child-care sector may offer certain services that compete well within the private market, but the private sector also has an unstable financial model. Because child-care programs make very little income, they typically pay their staff members poorly. In many cases, this means that a child-care program will have few, if any, highly qualified teachers. Also, most child-care programs operate close to their maximum capacity to collect all potential revenue. This means that they do not have the smaller class sizes and smaller adult-to-child ratios to accommodate children with special needs.

In the public sector of early childhood education, the public school system pays a higher wage and therefore can attract more qualified and experienced teachers. Also, public schools employ trained special-education staff who can work with children who have diagnosed disabilities or with children who need an evaluation. Unfortunately, the public school system typically allows parents to choose only the school that is closest to their home. They do not consider parent choice for early education. Also, hours of operation and style of curriculum may be limited.

With a significant difference in teacher education and pay between the public and the private school system, there can be significant differences in the quality of care and education that a child may receive between the private and public school system. However, children who qualify for a half-day of preschool with the public school system may have to turn down those services completely if their family needs to find full-day care to work. Children in low-income neighborhoods may have only one choice for preschool, particularly if transportation is an issue for the family, but children from high-income families may be able to offer their children access to one of many high-quality programs throughout the community. To better serve all families in the state or community, it is essential to find a way for the public and private sectors to work together.

PPPs are often categorized as "publicly funded, but privately provided" (Gustafsson-Wright, Smith, and Gardiner, 2017). Again, this means leveraging the state or federal funds to provide a service through a public entity. To help both organizations complete this type of partnership, there is usually a formal agreement such as a contract. The contract for mixed-delivery preschool typically includes points around the objectives for the private contractor, the payment structure, the quality and the quantity of the requirements, the operation period, and the shared risks (Gustafsson-Wright, Smith, and Gardiner, 2017). Some state governments are initially skeptical about giving state funds to a private entity; however, this type of contract is already in place for states with a child-care subsidy program. Private child-care programs are receiving public funds to cover the cost of tuition for a child who qualifies for child-care subsidy. Technically, the family qualifies for subsidy and then the family members decide where to use the subsidy. However, the private child-care program still has to participate in a formal agreement to meet the requirements listed in the Child Care and Development Block Grant to receive the subsidy for that child. If the program does not maintain the requirements, then it loses the ability to accept subsidy and the child will take the funding to another program. Consider Eric's story.

> I am a full-time working father, and my wife is enrolled in college full-time. We have two children, and my salary is not enough to cover all our expenses while my wife is in school, particularly the cost of child care for an infant and a three-year-old. Luckily, we qualify for the child-care assistance program in Kentucky. I went to the local office for the Department of Community-Based Services (DCBS), and I applied to get child-care assistance. It took several hours, and I had to bring a lot of mandatory

forms, including documentation of my income and proof that my wife is a full-time student. Once the paperwork was processed, we were awarded child-care assistance for one year for both of our children. Infant care is a lot more expensive than preschool, so my younger child received a higher amount of subsidy than my preschooler. The office gave me a certificate that says I am eligible for child-care assistance, but then I had to find a child-care program that had room for both of my children to enroll and that accepted a subsidy. Since the child-care program gets paid at the end of the month, instead of in advance, it seems that not every center wants to participate in the program. One center told me that there was too much paperwork to complete each month.

Once we found a program that could enroll both of our children, I had to contact the DCBS office again and tell them which center we chose so that they could send the money to the correct program. Even though my wife and I are the ones that qualify for the subsidy, we don't ever receive any of the money. It seems that the state subsidy system sends the child-care center an attendance form at the end of the month to ask what days my children attended, and once that is confirmed, then the state agency will pay the child-care program the tuition. The tuition for an infant is $225 a week at the program that we selected, but we will only receive $200 a week from the subsidy. My wife and I will have to pay the other $25 per week. The preschool classroom costs $190 per week, and the subsidy was $185 per week. We will have to pay the extra $5 per week. Overall, $30 per week is not a huge amount. Living on one income, that is really all we can afford to pay. Even though the state pays the child-care program at the end of the month, we still are responsible for paying the overage fee at the beginning of each week. Once my wife completes her degree, we will show our new income documentation and see if we still qualify for support. Since she will start off in an entry-level position, we may still get some amount of subsidy, but it won't be as much as we are receiving now.

When a private child-care program in the United States accepts public funding, it is typically through one of three ways (Gustafsson-Wright, Smith, and Gardiner, 2017):

- **Service-delivery model**—In this case, the government will subsidize a private service if an equivalent public service does not exist or if there is very limited access to it.
- **Voucher model**—A government voucher would cover the full cost of the private service.

- **Private management of public funds**—In this case, the government would pay a private contractor to manage and operate a service, such as public schools or child-care programs.

The child-care subsidy program may operate on the voucher model of PPPs. The voucher may not cover the full cost of child care (for private child-care programs that are extremely expensive), but it would cover a designated amount for each child who has a voucher and enrolls in a private program. In the mixed-delivery early education system, the service delivery model would be more appropriate. Access to state-funded preschool is limited, and the state cannot afford to build new buildings all over the state, not to mention find and train teachers for every location. So, when the state-funded preschool spots are full, the government partners with the private sector to provide families with additional access to high-quality early care and education.

PURPOSES OF PUBLIC-PRIVATE PARTNERSHIPS

When the state implements PPPs in early childhood education, there are several main purposes for those partnerships (Patrinos, 2023):

- To encourage innovation in the field
- To hold the schools accountable
- To empower the families
- To promote diversity

Private programs have become adept at solving problems simply to stay in business, but the state-funded preschool programs may not have had to create as many innovative ideas knowing they will receive state budget funds. When the two entities combine, it can create a lot of brainstorming on best practice with the state's data and the private sector's affinity for marketable ideas. Also, both industries can be held accountable in this partnership. First, parents will demand that the programs meet the quality and resources that their children need, so if one sector is offering better quality and customer service, the other sector will receive fewer requests for enrollment. Also, staff members will be looking at which system takes better care of its employees, and that sector will have lower teacher turnover and the fewest staffing openings.

Families are often empowered in the mixed-delivery early childhood education system by having choices (Patrinos, 2023). A family may choose the setting with the best supports for their child with special needs or the setting with the closest location to their employers. Either way, allowing families to have any choice at all helps them to feel more connected to their child's education system and allows them to demonstrate that the family knows the child the best. Partnership programs also promote diversity by making the providers of the service responsible to the clients, unlike many government models (Patrinos, 2023). Government employees may come predominantly from one background or one culture. When the mixed-delivery system allows private contractors to hire their own employees, there is typically a more diverse base of employees, and families may greatly value that diversity.

POSSIBLE CHALLENGES WITH PUBLIC-PRIVATE PARTNERSHIPS

When you ask private businesses and government agencies to partner together, there are some scenarios when those partnerships work better than others. Some private businesses may not want to partner with a government agency because they want to keep the business as independent as possible. Some school systems or government offices may not want to partner with a private business because it can be more challenging to supervise independent contractors than the agencies' own employees. Each organization may have initial misgivings about a partnership, but successful partnerships occur when both organizations place their bias aside to support the children and families in their local communities.

PPPs are most successful under several different sets of circumstances (Patrinos, 2023):

- When there is a lack of adequate supply
- When it is most cost effective for the budget
- When taking a systems approach
- When the private sector is allowed a considerable amount of autonomy

One of the issues for state-funded preschool is the ability to provide for every child who is eligible. If the only eligibility requirement is the child's age, such as in universal preschool, then the state needs to significantly expand its access. Families will be applying for spots, and large waiting lists will have to be created without a way to provide for more families. This is when most states initially consider mixed-delivery early childhood education: because they need to utilize every available asset in the state, even if that asset is privately funded. This partnership is also the most economic. Instead of building extra buildings and playgrounds, it seems most efficient to use the facilities that are already in place. Paying a per-child amount to an established quality child-care program is much more efficient than making huge capital investments and attempting to raise those funds.

When a state takes a systems approach to early childhood education, it is looking to address the underlying factors that could be a problem to the operational state system (Patrinos, 2023). In elementary schools, the state may identify the systems issues of underperforming schools. In early childhood education, it is more likely to identify hours of operation or government constraints on eligibility. These types of issues can be addressed for some families by enrolling in one of the partnering private child-care programs that offers full-day, full-year child care with government supports.

Child-care programs that are opposed to PPPs are typically worried about the loss of their autonomy, so if the partnership can be written with that flexibility in mind, then it should be much more successful. The government agency can set up a framework for accountability such as meeting state minimum requirements, but the government still should allow the private child care to manage its program independently (Patrinos, 2023). It is also critical for early childhood education programs to have academic flexibility as long as the students are achieving the developmental markers necessary to start kindergarten.

Patrinos (2023) also identifies trends on why early childhood education PPPs are not successful. Some of those reasons include the following:

- The partnership is based only on a shared facility, not on shared services.
- There is a lack of communication between the partners and the families.
- Accountability is not enforced.
- The state or community is not informed of the benefit.

An early childhood education mixed-delivery system comprises more than the school system using the physical space of one classroom at a private child-care facility. First, this type of arrangement is not collaborative. The public school is still conducting its own business, but it is just doing it in proximity to the private child-care business. A partnership involves much more than that. A true partnership is established through facility, funding, shared services, and even is detailed into professional development strategies in collaborative learning structures such as peer learning groups (Virginia Early Childhood Foundation, 2021; Griffey, 2019). If the collaboration is not present, then it isn't really a partnership.

PPPs can also fail if they lack a steady flow of communication between organizations and with families (Patrinos, 2023). Families should understand that they have more than one option so they can make an informed choice for their children. Private partners should be informed when new services are going to be offered just through the public partner or through both organizations. Miscommunication can cause mistrust and resentment, so stable communication must be in place.

If the public partner is responsible for offering the private funder the contract with the list of objectives and expectations, then it is essential for measures to be in place for the public funder to hold the private partner accountable. If the contract requires certain services from the private funder, then the public partner needs to audit those services. Partnerships can easily fall apart when there is no accountability. If one partner knows it will never be asked to prove that it is meeting the objectives, then it will feel much less motivated to complete the required tasks. That will lead to a collapse in quality.

When states or cities create these amazing mixed-delivery programs to serve families, it is essential to market the programs to the public. Many families don't even know where in their state to direct questions to find out about programs like mixed-delivery child care. Very few will go looking for information on a state website or do background research. If the state wants the new program to be successful, they must market the program to families. This means that the audience of the marketing materials must be adults caring for young children. Materials need to be shared at doctors' offices, the public library, and areas of the communities to which these families go. When the program is later reviewed at the state level, the community does not want the program to be cut due to lack of interest simply because families were unaware.

Even though state-funded preschool programs look very different from state to state, each state has an opportunity to make its mixed-delivery program successful. The key ingredient is simply leveraging state funds to create early childhood services that can benefit a wide variety of families.

Since public and private partnerships for early childhood education have some flexibility in the way that they are implemented, different states have decided to implement their systems in a variety of ways. Some states try to use a model similar to Early Head Start partnerships, but others design a system specific to their state and its needs. If a state is considering using partnerships, looking at successful state models that are already implemented can be the first place to start in order to see what methods have already been successful.

CHAPTER 7

State Models of Mixed-Delivery Early Childhood Education

When a state, or a city, decides to implement a mixed-delivery early childhood system, it is important to learn from communities that have already worked on the model and had successes or failures. Each state that has set up a mixed-delivery preschool model runs its program slightly differently. Some mandate that a portion of state preschool funds must be used outside the public school system; others need partnerships with local child-care programs to serve all the children who would like to enroll in the program. Some states focus their prekindergarten (pre-K) programs on families whose incomes are below the federal poverty level or for children with disabilities, while others use a lottery system to make the available slots open to any family who is interested. Some states focus on full-day prekindergarten, and others have the funding for only half-day programs. Each state individualizes its program based on its needs and its resources.

Administration of the prekindergarten systems is diverse as well. Some states have their department of education directly supervise the prekindergarten program. Other states have local school boards or coalitions act as an intermediaries. Some states do a per-child funding amount based on enrollment and full-day/half-day status, while other states use a formula to calculate a per-child or flat-rate amount based on a previous year's enrollment. Each of these methods has advantages and challenges. Seeing how a variety of states run their mixed-delivery preschool programs can be a huge help to other states trying to plan for their future preschool programs. In the remainder of this chapter, we will look at early childhood programs in seven states—Alabama, Florida, Michigan, New Jersey, New York, Oklahoma, and West Virginia—to learn how different states implement the mixed-delivery approach.

ALABAMA

Alabama began its first state-funded prekindergarten programs in 2001, but its current program, First Class Pre-K (FCPK), was created during the 2008–2009 school year. During the 2020–2021 school year, Alabama served 18,906 four-year-old children in its preschool program (Garver et al., 2023). That was only 31 percent of the eligible four-year-old children throughout the state. Eighty-two percent of the children served received preschool services through the local school district, and 18 percent of the children received pre-K through a mixed-delivery setting that received public funding through the school system. A higher percentage of low-income students were served in mixed-delivery settings, including Head Start programs. Also, state data show that a higher percentage of Black students were served in mixed-delivery settings.

ADMINISTRATION

Alabama's FCPK is administered at the state level by the Office of School Readiness in the Alabama Department of Early Childhood Education (Garver et al., 2023). The state determines which families are eligible to participate. The state Department of Education identifies the areas of the state that need additional preschool classrooms, and then regional staff members, such as early childhood specialists or coaches, recruit potential classrooms from Head Start programs, private schools, or child-care programs that can participate in the FCPK program. The regional staff members are responsible for recruiting in both English and Spanish. There is not a legislative statute requiring mixed delivery, but public schools and other forms of child care are allowed to apply to the state to become part of the FCPK system.

FUNDING

New classrooms participating in FCPK receive $150,000 the first year and must have all eighteen students by the end of the first two weeks of school (Garver et al., 2023). If the classroom continues to participate in the program, it will receive a minimum amount of $50,400 per year in the following years, but there is a possibility for the classroom to receive up to $100,008, including a per-child amount if higher numbers of low-income students are enrolled in the program. Seventy-five percent of funding comes from Alabama's Education Trust Fund budget, but local communities are required to contribute a 25-percent match to the program.

ELIGIBILITY

There are no income-eligibility requirements for families who want to apply to the program (Garver et al., 2023). Families can preregister on the state's online system, and they can preregister for more than one location, allowing them some level of choice in the type of program and the location they prefer. If there is more interest in enrollment than there are spots available, then the grantee (public school or private entity) must have a public drawing to see who will receive the available spots. Families whose names are drawn must accept or decline the spot, and then the other names are placed on a waitlist.

STAFF TRAINING

Alabama attempts to keep educator/staff requirements similar across settings in the mixed-delivery system (Garver et al., 2023). All lead teachers must have a bachelor's degree in the field of early childhood education, child development, or a similar degree. Teachers who work in the public school system must also have a teacher's certification in early education. Assistant teachers must have a minimum of a CDA certificate or nine hours of early childhood education coursework from a higher education program. Both teachers and assistant teachers are required to receive twenty hours of professional development training each year to continue learning in their field.

STAFF SALARIES

With the attempt to keep education and training levels similar across education settings, Alabama's FCPK also requests commensurate pay for teachers throughout the system (Garver et al., 2023). In the 2020–2021 school year, prekindergarten teachers in the public school system averaged an annual salary of $49,866 per year, and teachers in Head Start and private prekindergarten classrooms averaged an annual salary of $42,734. There is probably some fluctuation of the average based on the number of years a teacher has been in the public school system compared to the number of years a teacher has served in a private setting. The annual salary for a kindergarten teacher in Alabama during the 2020–2021 school year was $49,100. Although FCPK asked for commensurate salary for prekindergarten teachers, it did not ask for mandates on staff benefits; those are determined by the grantee.

GUIDELINES AND ASSESSMENT

Along with teacher salary, FCPK determined other guidelines for participating prekindergarten programs (Garver et al., 2023). The state programs utilize a staff-to-child ratio of one to ten in prekindergarten classrooms with a maximum group size of twenty students. Also, the school day must last for at least six and a half hours; however, the grantee could determine the number of hours beyond the minimum. Classrooms are assessed with the *Classroom Assessment* scoring tool (McMillan, 2004) and the *Early Childhood Environmental Rating Scale,* 3rd edition (Harms, Clifford, and Cryer, 2014). Early childhood specialists from the state assess the classrooms with these tools twice a year, in addition to planned and random site visits to ensure quality and accountability. Programs in the FCPK program do not have to participate in the state's Quality Rating and Improvement System (QRIS) program but are encouraged to do so.

FLORIDA

Florida began state-funded preschool options in the 1990s. In 2005, it created its Voluntary Prekindergarten Education Program, also known as VPK (Friedman-Krauss et al., 2022). This program has three separate components: a school-year program, a summer program, and a specialized instructional services program that focuses on four-year-olds with disabilities in nontraditional settings. The school-year program includes 540 hours of instructional time, a maximum classroom size of twenty, and a one-to-eleven or two-to-twenty adult-to-child ratio (Alawsaj, Berman, Mujaj, and Rankin, 2023).

The teacher for the school-year program must have a minimum education level of a CDA credential. Assistant teachers are required to have a high school diploma or an equivalent.

The summer program includes 300 instructional hours, a one-to-twelve adult-to-child ratio, a maximum classroom size of twelve, and a teacher with a bachelor's degree in the field of early education (Alawsaj, Berman, Mujaj, and Rankin, 2023).

ADMINISTRATION

Any early education program in Florida can apply to be a part of the VPK. Certain requirements must be in place to be a part of the program, but all applications can be considered. Although the state offers the contracts to the early education programs that participate in the program, one of the thirty early learning coalitions positioned throughout Florida will oversee all the preschool classrooms in the program (Friedman-Krauss et al., 2022). Instead of having only one governing body of child care in Florida, there are coalitions in charge of early childhood education governance. These coalitions are regional, so the supervision is localized (Alawsaj, Berman, Mujaj, and Rankin, 2023).

FUNDING

In 2020, Florida served 166,726 four-year-olds in the VPK program, which was 72 percent of the eligible children. The state awarded $2,222 per pupil during 2020, which was down from $3,224 per pupil in 2008 (Friedman-Krauss et al., 2022). With this amount of funding, the local administration can determine what the hours of operation are for each classroom and whether the program operates during the school year only or also during the summer (Alawsaj, Berman, Mujaj, and Rankin, 2023). Once programs accept the $2,222 per-pupil fee, they are not permitted to charge the families any additional amount of tuition.

MICHIGAN

Michigan currently has two preschool programs, but the Great Start Readiness Program (GSRP) mandates a mixed-delivery system. The program was established to support low-income families, and 90 percent of the enrollment is reserved for families with an income that is at or below 250 percent of the Federal Poverty Level (Garver et al., 2023). During the 2020–2021 school year, 26,775 four-year-olds were served in the GSRP, and that was only 31 percent of the eligible four-year-olds in the state. Forty-one percent of those four-year-olds were served in an early education classroom outside the public school system. GSRP requires that at least 30 percent of the children enrolled be in preschool classrooms outside the public school setting.

ADMINISTRATION

The Michigan Department of Education, Office of Preschool and Out-of-School Time Learning, supervises the GSRP (Garver et al., 2023); however, the preschool classrooms in the program are supervised by Michigan's Intermediate School Districts (ISDs). There are fifty-six of these regional education offices throughout the state, similar to the way that some states have county boards of education. The ISD offices contract with the public school preschool classrooms, Head Start classrooms, and private child-care programs that are all a part of the GSRP. Based on the need in each area, the ISD may need to recruit Head Start and private child-care programs to partner with the district. The ISDs are also responsible for program compliance for the prekindergarten classrooms.

FUNDING

Once a prekindergarten classroom is part of the GSRP, it must prioritize low-income families in the enrollment process (Garver et al., 2023). Michigan uses one enrollment application for state and federally funded early education programs that include GSRP and the Head Start system. This helps families spend less time filling out paperwork at multiple agencies while trying to find a classroom with available enrollment. The state issues a per-child amount to the prekindergarten classrooms of $8,700 per year for a child attending a full-day program and $4,350 per year for a child attending a half-day program (Garver et al., 2023). Michigan also sets aside an additional $10 million appropriation to fund transportation for these programs, and this money is disbursed based on the need for transporting children to and from the classroom.

STAFFING

Staff salaries and benefits for the GSRP teachers are set by the ISD, not the state, so there could be some variability based on region (Garver et al., 2023). All lead teachers must have a four-year degree in the field of early childhood education, or they must be enrolled in a four-year program and able to finish within two years of being hired. Assistant teachers must have a two-year degree in early childhood education or a CDA certification. If either of these credentials is not complete, the assistant teacher has the option to be enrolled in the program with the ability to finish within two years. All members of the teaching staff must receive sixteen hours of continuing education courses each year to advance in the field, and they are also assigned an early childhood coach from the ISD for mentoring and training purposes.

GSRP does not require pay parity for its teaching staff (Garver et al., 2023). During the 2020–2021 school year, the average salary for a GSRP lead teacher in a public school was $43,505, and the average salary for a GSRP lead teacher in a Head Start or private child-care setting was $33,051. These two salaries were significantly lower than the average salary for a kindergarten teacher that year in Michigan, which was $59,910 (Garver et al., 2023).

GUIDELINES AND ASSESSMENT

GSRP requires prekindergarten classrooms to be open at least three hours a day four days per week (Garver et al., 2023). Many programs may choose to operate more than the minimum hours required, but some programs may be limited to the minimum hours due to the amount of funding provided. The adult-to-child ratio in the classroom is one to eight, and the maximum classroom size is eighteen children.

Classrooms are assessed annually by the ISD office using the *Classroom Assessment* scoring tool (McMillan, 2004) and the *Program Quality Assessment—R* (HighScope Educational Research Foundation, 2019). The ISD coaches are trained in how to use the scoring tools effectively and will assess the classrooms during the annual visits. Prekindergarten classrooms in GSRP are required to participate in Michigan's Quality Rating and Improvement System (QRIS), and coaches at the ISD can guide the classrooms through that process.

NEW JERSEY

New Jersey has three separate preschool programs, but it is phasing out two of the programs and focusing time and materials on the Preschool Expansion Program (Garver et al., 2023). New Jersey's state-funded preschool also includes the Abbott Preschool Program, which was created after the New Jersey Supreme Court cases collectively referred to as *Abbott v. Burke*. In this case, the court ruled against the state funding formula for low-income neighborhoods. The court case initially focused on twenty-eight districts, but it eventually expanded to thirty-one. In those districts, the state must offer free, high-quality preschool. The court also required the public school districts to collaborate with Head Start programs and private child-care programs.

ADMINISTRATION

During the 2020–2021 school year, New Jersey served 46,895 preschool students, which was 29 percent of eligible four-year-olds and 3 percent of eligible three-year-olds (Garver et al., 2023). Fifty-nine percent of the preschool students were served in the public school system, and 41 percent were served in other settings such as Head Start and private child care. The state Department of Education is the administrator of the mixed-delivery preschool program; however, the public school system is the supervisor of the public school preschool classrooms and of the classrooms in alternative settings. The public school districts subcontract with Head Start programs, private schools, and private child care that are a part of the Preschool Expansion Program.

The public school districts work with a liaison from the Department of Education to plan budget review and programming (Garver et al., 2023). The school districts are also responsible for recruiting partner classrooms that are willing and able to be a part of the Preschool Expansion Program. The public school programs are required to contract with classrooms outside of the public school system, but they are not required to partner with every classroom that applies. If a prekindergarten program applies and does not meet the quality requirements, the New Jersey QRIS coaches will work with the classroom to improve the level of quality to allow them to participate.

FUNDING

New Jersey's Preschool Expansion Program offers different per-pupil amounts for public school classrooms, Head Start classrooms, and private child-care classrooms with consideration to what other types of funding those programs may be receiving (Garver et al., 2023). The public school classroom will receive $11,506 per child per year, and the Head Start classrooms will receive $7,146 per child per year. The private child-care programs receive the largest amount of $12,934 per child per year because they are the most financially fragile. All prekindergarten classrooms accepted into the program will have the proposed budget included in their contract, and the contract will state when the payments will be made. Classrooms are responsible for tracking finances and adjusting budgets for under-enrollment.

STAFFING

Lead teachers must have a four-year degree in the field and a teacher certification in early childhood education. If the teacher's certification is in a different education area, the teacher needs at least two years' experience with prekindergarten. Assistant teachers are required to have a high school diploma. All teaching staff are required to have twenty hours of professional development per year and/or one hundred hours of training in a five-year period.

All teachers in the Preschool Expansion Program are required to have the same starting salary, salary schedule, paid time off, and paid professional development training. The salaries are all set to a 180-day school year. The programs outside the public school system are not required to have benefits parity. Adult-to-child ratios for the preschool classroom are two adults to fifteen children, and the maximum classroom size is fifteen children. The school day must be at least six hours long.

ASSESSMENT

All new prekindergarten classrooms must be a part of the QRIS system, but the Abbott prekindergarten classrooms are not required to be a part of the QRIS. The public school system will monitor all prekindergarten classrooms at least once a year. No specific assessment tool is required for the monitoring visit, but classroom observations and the visit specialists will make sure that all requirements in the contract are being met. The public school system will be monitored by the state department of education every three years.

NEW YORK

New York serves more than 50 percent of its four-year-old children in its two prekindergarten programs: Universal Prekindergarten (UPK) and Statewide Universal Full-Day Prekindergarten (SUFDPK) (Garver et al., 2023). The programs are similar in their overall requirements; however, UPK focuses on half-day classrooms, and SUFDPK focuses on full-day classrooms. The half-day program must serve at least 2.5 hours per day, and the full-day program must serve at least five hours per day. SUFDPK focuses on four-year-old students, and UPK is for three-year-old and four-year-old children.

New York began its quest for universal prekindergarten in 2014; in 2021, 115,596 children enrolled in the state's prekindergarten program. Forty-six percent of four-year-olds and 6 percent of three-year-olds are enrolled in the program (Garver et al., 2023). Due to the number of children accessing prekindergarten, 59 percent of children enrolled in New York's prekindergarten program are in classrooms outside the public school system. There are no income eligibility requirements for students to participate in the program.

ADMINISTRATION

The Office of Early Learning at the New York Department of Education is the administrative authority for the UPK and SUFDPK programs (Garver et al., 2023). The Department of Education asks the public school system to recruit Head Start programs and private child-care programs to participate in the programs and to supervise the classrooms admitted. However, the state will work directly with Head Start programs and private child-care programs if the local school districts choose not to partner with them.

Ten percent of the funding for both prekindergarten programs must go toward mixed-delivery partnerships. The local school districts put out the applications for community programs such as Head Starts and child-care programs to apply to be in the UPK or SUFDPK programs. The state requires that there be at least one site visit to the applicant's facility before it is accepted into the program, and the contracting prekindergarten classroom must be in the same district as the supervising public school district. The same enrollment application is used for all prekindergarten classrooms, including the public school classrooms.

FUNDING

The per-child amount of funding is determined by the public school district and the contracting prekindergarten classroom (Garver et al., 2023). The minimum amount of per-child funding is $5,400 per year. In the SUFDPK program, the per-child amount can be $10,000 per child if the teacher is certified or $7,000 with an uncertified teacher. All prekindergarten classrooms must create an annual budget, and the public school districts must monitor and oversee the classroom budgets. Classrooms in the UPK and SFDUPK programs cannot charge parents in addition to the state funding amount, so the budget must be set up accurately. Department of Education staff may do some program monitoring and evaluation on top of the assessment completed by the local school districts.

STAFFING

State law requires that lead teachers must not only have a four-year degree and a teacher's certification but also must obtain a master's degree within five years (Garver et al., 2023). This requirement is in place for all lead teachers, not just those in the public school system. Lead teachers must also obtain 175 hours of professional development within a five-year time period. Assistant teachers in a public school classroom must have an assistant teacher certification. All other assistant teachers must have a high school diploma or equivalent. The New York prekindergarten system does not require pay parity; however, union negotiations require pay parity for teachers within the state. Prekindergarten classrooms in the UPK and SFDUPK programs must achieve an adult-to-child ratio of one to nine with a maximum classroom size of twenty students (Garver et al., 2023).

ASSESSMENT

All classrooms must participate in New York's QRIS rating system. The public school district is responsible for making sure that all prekindergarten classrooms are compliant with state mandates. Each classroom will have an annual visit from the state, and the assessor will complete New York's Quality Assurance Protocol when observing the classroom setting.

OKLAHOMA

In the 2020–2021 school year, Oklahoma served 42,683 children in its prekindergarten program (Alawsaj, Berman, Mujaj, and Rankin, 2023). That number included 70 percent of the eligible four-year-olds and 5 percent of the eligible three-year-olds.

Children could enroll in a full-day or half-day classroom. The minimum period of operation is two and a half hours per day, at least five days per week (Friedman-Krauss et al., 2022). The per-child reimbursement rate is $4,643 per year. There are no family income eligibility requirements to apply for preschool. All funding operates on the academic school year, but programs can still choose to operate on a year-round basis.

Oklahoma requires pay parity for public school lead preschool teachers compared to kindergarten to third grade teachers, but there is no pay parity in place for Head Start or private child-care teachers who are a part of the mixed-delivery system. Lead teachers for the public school system in the Oklahoma mixed-delivery preschool program must have a four-year degree and an early childhood teacher certification (Alawsaj, Berman, Mujaj, and Rankin, 2023). Their average annual salary is $53,341. Assistant teachers must have a high school diploma (Friedman-Krauss et al., 2022). All teaching staff must receive fifteen hours of professional development training per year. The classroom curriculum must meet Oklahoma Standards for Accreditation and Oklahoma Academic Standards. For three-year-old prekindergarten students, the adult-to-child ratio is one to nine, and the maximum classroom size is eighteen. For four-year-old students, the adult-to-child ratio is one to ten, and the maximum classroom size is twenty.

WEST VIRGINIA

West Virginia established its prekindergarten program in 2002. In 2014, legislation was passed that ensured all fifty-five counties would have free prekindergarten for all four-year-olds and for all three-year-olds with a diagnosed disability (Garver et al., 2023). The legislation required cooperation among the public school system, Head Start, and child-care programs, and it mandated that 50 percent of the prekindergarten classrooms would be mixed delivery. In the 2020–2021 school year, West Virginia served 11,981 children in the mixed-delivery prekindergarten program (Friedman-Krauss et al., 2022). In the 2019–2020 school year, 68 percent of four-year-olds and 6 percent of eligible three-year-olds were attending West Virginia's prekindergarten program.

ADMINISTRATION

The Department of Education, Division of Teaching and Learning, is the administrative authority for the universal prekindergarten system, but policy is set by the West Virginia Pre-K Steering Team (Garver et al., 2023). The steering team is composed of the Department of Education; the Department of Health and Human Services, which oversees the Child Care and Development Block Grant funds for child care;

and the Head Start collaboration office. This same state structure also occurs at the local level. Each of the fifty-five counties has a local County Collaborative Early Childhood Core Team. These local teams oversee the prekindergarten program as an intermediary between the individual classrooms and the state. They are responsible for data collection, financial oversight, and reporting. They are also responsible for recruiting the Head Start programs and private child-care programs to partner with the local state-funded preschool programs. The core teams also make sure that at least 50 percent of the prekindergarten classrooms are mixed delivery.

The public school system is the fiscal agent in each county (Garver et al., 2023). The core team develops a county-wide enrollment process based on the minimum state standards. The core team is also responsible for coming up with a funding formula that is based on the previous year's enrollment on October 1. After completing the funding formula, the core team must complete a budget and a cost-allocation worksheet to outline expected costs and resources for the documented school year. Each county's prekindergarten coordinator for the public school system is responsible for fiscal monitoring for all prekindergarten classrooms in the county (Garver et al., 2023).

The county is required to provide at least twenty-five hours of care per week over at least four days per school week (Garver et al., 2023). The adult-to-child ratio is one to ten, and the maximum classroom size is twenty. Parents can be charged for hours outside of the twenty-five hours per school week, but the twenty-five hours is paid for through the fiscal agent. Currently, 82 percent of the prekindergarten classrooms in West Virginia are mixed delivery (Garver et al., 2023).

STAFFING

Lead teachers in the West Virginia universal prekindergarten system must have a four-year degree (Garver et al., 2023). Lead teachers in the public school system must also have a teacher's certification in early childhood education. The other lead teachers, if needed, can have a West Virginia Community Program Permanent Authorization, which is a credential requiring the teacher to have earned an associate's degree in early childhood, child development, or occupational development with an emphasis in early childhood/child development and eighteen hours of college coursework, instead of a teacher's certification. Assistant teachers must have a minimum of a CDA certification. All teaching staff must have a minimum of fifteen hours of professional development training per year in order to continue learning about their field.

Lead teachers and assistant teachers in the public school system must have pay parity with their equivalent staff members in the K–12 classrooms, but there are no requirements for pay parity for lead teachers and assistant teachers in the Head Start or private child-care programs.

ASSESSMENT

The local core team is responsible for monitoring compliance with all of the prekindergarten classrooms in their counties (Garver et al., 2023). The classrooms are not required to participate in a QRIS system. Instead, the core team will use three data sources to monitor fidelity: the West Virginia Pre-K Health and Safety Checklist, county-level child-outcome data, and classroom observation data. The state will inspect all classrooms every three years.

DECISIONS FOR MIXED-DELIVERY IMPLEMENTATION

With all of these different models of mixed-delivery implementation, it is essential for each state to ask some specific questions before designing its mixed-delivery model:

- Which organization is the administrative authority?
- Will the classrooms be assessed for compliance at the local or the state level?
- Which organization will be responsible for recruiting Head Start and private child-care programs to partner with state-funded prekindergarten?
- Which organization determines the funding level, and will funding be the same across the state?
- Is legislation required to design and implement the program?
- What are the required teacher qualifications?
- Is pay parity necessary across all classroom settings?
- What type of professional development and mentoring is available to teachers?
- Is there one coordinated enrollment system that supports families looking for early education?
- Will all families have equitable access to high-quality child care based on the system that is going to be set in place?

When you look at the characteristics of states that have been successful with mixed delivery, you see common themes such as a unified application system and parity with program quality across settings. Cities and states considering creating their own systems must think about these themes. It is also important for states to consider which children they plan on serving through the mixed-delivery system. Will it be all three-year-old and four-year-old students, or is the goal simply to serve more students than are currently enrolled in public-school preschool? When communities decide to serve all preschool students, then the discussion turns toward universal prekindergarten.

CHAPTER 8

Universal Preschool Compared to Mixed-Delivery Care

Once cities and states begin to look at implementing a mixed-delivery model for early childhood education, it is important to decide which children they will be serving and how many children they have the capacity to serve.

DEFINING UNIVERSAL PRE-K AND MIXED-DELIVERY PRESCHOOL

Some states use the terms *universal pre-K* and *mixed-delivery preschool* interchangeably, but it is important to understand that there are differences in the terminology. As defined in chapter 5, mixed-delivery preschool is when two of the three models (federally funded preschool [Head Start], state-funded preschool, and private child care) partner to create a more enhanced early childhood experience (Early Care and Education Consortium, 2021). A mixed-delivery model can be used for universal pre-K, but many states use mixed-delivery early education without universal access.

The Alliance for Early Success (2022) defines *universal pre-K* as "pre-K for all." This definition really speaks to eligibility and capacity more than any other characteristics. States and cities would have to choose among a lot of variables before implementing universal preschool, including the following:

- Where would funding for universal pre-K come from (federal, state, or local)?
- Will universal pre-K be available to three-year-olds, four-year-olds, or both?
- Will early education programs outside of the public school system be able to participate in the universal pre-K program?

The National Institute for Early Education Research (NIEER) defines universal pre-K slightly differently, but the overall intent is the same. In its definition, NIEER says that age would be the only eligibility criterion (Barnett and Gomez, 2016). It also says that any child who wants to enroll would have the opportunity to do so, just like enrolling in the K–12 school system.

States that do not have the capacity to allow every child to enroll would establish a lottery for the enrollment slots. When states look at the percentage of preschool-aged children from their state enrolled in pre-K, the marker for "universal" pre-K is typically 70 percent enrollment or higher, knowing that not all families will choose to participate in the voluntary program (Friedman-Krauss et al., 2022). With those characteristics in mind, the definition of universal pre-K for any state or community could include the following:

- Children are eligible by age, not by family income level.
- All children within the age range can have an enrollment slot in the universal pre-K program.
- Seventy percent or more of eligible children enroll in the universal pre-K system.

Capacity to serve more children is one of the major factors to consider when deciding to move to a universal pre-K program. It can take several years to build the capacity to serve up to 70 percent of the eligible children in the state. NIEER's *The State of Preschool 2021* (Friedman-Krauss et al., 2022) describes several states with strong mixed-delivery preschool programs that were trying to increase capacity to a universal pre-K level. They were already serving 45 percent or more of the state's eligible preschool children, but they still had to make strides to increase access. Those states included Arkansas, California, Georgia, Louisiana, Maine, Maryland, New Mexico, New York, South Carolina, and Texas. Other states have bipartisan support for preschool expansion, but it will take years to grow their current mixed-delivery system.

There is some amount of confusion related to the term *universal* when discussing universal pre-K. It is often interpreted as "mandatory." Although a true universal pre-K system would make it mandatory for the state to offer pre-K to eligible children, universal pre-K is not mandatory for eligible children to attend. Many families in each state may still choose to keep their children at home with a family member until starting kindergarten. And some families will choose to pay for private child care instead of participating in the state-funded universal pre-K program.

A state can have a universal pre-K program open to all eligible children and still have significant differences from other state programs. Some of the variables that are unique to each state for universal pre-K include the following:

- Hours of operation (currently ranging from ten hours per week to full-day care and education)
- Per-child funding amount (currently $2,200 to $15,000 annually, depending on the state)
- Mixed-delivery model or strictly in the public school system
- Teacher-education requirements and compensation
- Classroom ratios and sizes
- Traditional school calendar or year-round care and education

NIEER HIGH-QUALITY PRESCHOOL BENCHMARKS

Because government funding at both the state and federal levels can be very limiting, the quality of universal pre-K can be limited. One great concern for many states is that opening access to pre-K for more children will cause the quality of the care and education to significantly decrease due to limited funds. Until more funding is available, it may be more beneficial to the state's children to offer a high-quality program with narrower eligibility instead of drastically reducing quality.

As mentioned in chapter 2, each year NIEER rates every state program against a list of high-quality benchmarks, whether or not the program is universal. In 2021, three of the fifty states were able to meet all ten benchmarks on their assessment, although other states received scores as high as 9.6 (Friedman-Krauss et al., 2022). In general, states scored the highest on having early learning and development standards, but many of the states struggled with credentials and professional development training for teachers and assistant teachers. Understanding and implementing the benchmark standards can help strengthen universal pre-K in each state.

- **Early learning and development standards**—This benchmark means that each state has a comprehensive set of early learning and development standards that are supported by the state administration and show cultural sensitivity to a wide variety of families.

- **Curriculum supports**—This means that the state would offer support for programs to select an appropriate curriculum and help the classroom implement the curriculum once it is selected.
- **Bachelor's degree for lead teachers**—The lead teacher in the classroom will have completed a bachelor's degree at a four-year higher education program, preferably in the field of early education.
- **Teachers have specialized training in pre-K**—Instead of having a degree in elementary education or a related field, this benchmark means that lead teachers are specifically trained in how to work with children from birth through kindergarten.
- **Assistant teachers have CDA certificates**—Assistant teachers will have a CDA certificate through the Council for Professional Recognition or the equivalent to that level of education.
- **Staff professional development**—This benchmark refers to ongoing professional development once the teacher is already teaching in the classroom. Both lead teachers and assistant teachers should receive a minimum of fifteen clock hours of professional development training per year. Also, the teaching staff should have access to coaching/mentoring staff and have an individualized professional development plan to set and achieve new goals.
- **Class size**—Maximum class size of twenty
- **Ratios**—Adult-to-child ratio of one to ten or smaller
- **Screening and referral process for children with suspected delays**—Children should have access to vision and hearing screenings. Also, if a developmental delay is suspected, the program should have access to refer the child for a developmental evaluation.
- **Continuous quality improvement system**—This goal requires that classrooms are observed on an established schedule for feedback. It also requires a program to collect key data about the program. Together, the data and observation information can be used to make decisions to help the program continue to improve over time.

A number of policy changes and funding are still needed for all states to meet these benchmarks. A lot of the additional cost is associated with salaries to compensate qualified teachers. Another large cost is associated with maintaining adult-to-child ratios and maximum classroom sizes that can ensure safety while providing the individualized instruction that the children need to be as successful as possible.

NIEER'S PLAN FOR UNIVERSAL PRE-K

To establish a goal for the United States as a whole, NIEER created a plan to achieve universal pre-K for the nation as a whole by the year 2050 (NIEER, 2021a). The plan establishes that each state would offer a minimum of a 180-day school year with full-day classes lasting a minimum of six hours per day. The per-child amount offered annually would be $12,500. The state would also be responsible for paying a competitive salary for teachers. With this plan, all states would be responsible for meeting all ten benchmarks for high-quality preschool.

The cost of care would be based on a cost-modeling scale instead of market-rate value (NIEER, 2021a). The expansion from limited preschool accessibility to nationwide universal pre-K would move from 1.5 million children to, eventually, approximately 5 million children. The first phase of the NIEER plan would be to open eligibility for state-funded preschool to all children who are three or four years old whose families are at 200 percent of the Federal Poverty Level. Then, by the year 2025, the eligibility would open to all three- and four-year-old children. This type of investment in early care and education would require the states and federal governments to participate in a fifty–fifty match on funding.

The goal of implementing universal pre-K is to provide a high-quality early childhood education to young children so that they can be as successful as possible when entering the kindergarten classroom. It is also critical for a high-quality early childhood environment to assist the development of the whole child, including social, emotional, and physical domains, and not just pre-academic skills. To make sure that children receive a high-quality early education experience, several factors must be present:

- Highly qualified early childhood educators
- A developmentally appropriate learning environment
- Small classroom sizes to allow teachers to spend time with each child
- Ongoing coaching and training for teachers
- A referral process for special-education services for children with delays

These services create a supportive environment that will allow the child to have a positive early learning experience, but they can also affect the cost and implementation of universal pre-K.

CHALLENGES OF UNIVERSAL PRE-K

In the remainder of this chapter, we look at several of the challenges of universal preschool, including the cost and supply of staffing; its impact on private child-care programs, in particular infant and toddler care; adequate funding and support on a state-wide level; and providing developmentally appropriate practice and child care when families need it.

COST AND SUPPLY OF STAFFING

One of the largest considerations for universal pre-K is the cost and supply of staffing. To find highly qualified teachers to work with children with and without disabilities, it is essential to pay those teachers a professional salary (Sullivan, 2021). Since universal pre-K may be distributed through a mixed-delivery system to public schools, Head Start classrooms, and private child-care programs, it is important to think about how all teachers in the universal pre-K program need to be paid an equitable wage for doing the same job. If universal pre-K teachers are paid a competitive wage only when they work in the public school building, it will be incredibly difficult to find teachers to lead classrooms in the community partner facilities.

Once all the universal pre-K teachers are receiving a competitive salary, the mixed-delivery facilities (Head Start programs and private child-care programs) have to consider how that affects the rest of their staff members. If infant and toddler teachers are paid a significantly lower wage than preschool teachers, it could cause complications for the early education facilities. First, a lower pay rate could make it hard to recruit teachers to work in infant and toddler classrooms. Potential teachers could purposely look for pre-K positions simply for the salary. Second, a pay differentiation could cause tension among staff members who feel that they are getting paid less for doing the same job as their co-workers. The biggest problem that this pay discrepancy causes is the image that infant and toddler care is not as important as preschool care, so those teachers do not need to be paid as much.

The ultimate solution to this problem is working toward the goal of all early childhood educators receiving a competitive salary so qualified teachers do not leave the field to work in higher-paying professions. Unfortunately, this is a process that is going to take multiple steps. First, the public school preschool teachers need to achieve pay parity with their K–12 colleagues. Then, the universal pre-K teachers in the private sector need to receive salary and benefit parity with their public-school colleagues. Finally, it is essential that the infant and toddler teachers receive pay parity with their preschool teacher colleagues. As this process evolves, it is going to cause a ripple of inflation due to the need for additional funding for staff salaries.

It is a necessary part of the process to obtain a high-quality early education system, but the strain on funding will be an obstacle.

IMPACT ON PRIVATE CHILD CARE

Another challenge for implementing universal pre-K is making sure that private child care in the state does not collapse when universal pre-K is implemented. If the public school system decides to expand to serve 70 percent or more of the eligible preschool students in the state, many of those preschool students will be pulled out of child-care programs, leaving significant gaps in enrollment and income in the private child-care programs. Housing all the preschool students in the public school system will also require the system to expand its facilities with additional capital projects to accommodate all the new students and hire teachers and assistant teachers to work with the preschoolers.

While the public school system is spending money on building new classrooms, the private child-care field will retain only infants and toddlers, and all child-care programs lose funding from caring for infants and toddlers because the adult-to-child ratio is too low to cover the cost of staffing. If private child care is losing money, business owners will most likely decide to close their doors, and the ramifications of those closings will have a ripple effect (Mueller and Sutton, 2023). If a program closes, the child-care providers lose their jobs. If those child-care providers do not qualify for a position with the public school system due to education level or years of experience, they will have a difficult time finding re-employment.

The closure of private child-care programs will eliminate a huge portion of infant and toddler care in the state. A significant lack of infant or toddler care could prevent many mothers from reentering the workforce after their maternity leave. If a family cannot find safe and affordable child care, often one family member will have to make the tough decision to stay home with the child or change jobs to work more convenient hours for the family's schedule. More often than not, it is the mother who makes the decision to stay home and take care of her child (Goldberg, 2020). In a single-parent family, this decision can be extremely detrimental. It can limit the family's ability to obtain safe housing, adequate food, and reliable transportation. It can also cause the family to rely on multiple government assistance programs to get the basic necessities for survival. Once a caregiver leaves the workforce for several years, it can be difficult to re-enter at the previous level of pay. This can mean that the family will still suffer from unstable resources.

ADEQUATE FUNDING ON A STATEWIDE LEVEL

For universal pre-K to be a successful venture in any state, it really must be an "all-in" policy. It is not going to benefit young children if the state does not back the program wholeheartedly. For example, a state that designs a universal pre-K program but attempts to spend as little as possible on staffing is not going to be successful. Qualified teachers are not going to take a pay cut to work in the universal pre-K system. In this type of scenario, pre-K classrooms will end up with entry-level staff members who do not have the needed education or experience to be successful.

A pre-K classroom with twenty or more children is challenging for even an experienced teacher, but it can be emotionally overwhelming for untrained or inexperienced staff members. Unfortunately, when staff members are emotionally overwhelmed, the children are the ones who end up suffering (Gray, 2021). Stressed teachers inadvertently take out their frustrations in the classroom, and children become just as stressed as the adults. Classrooms in which children feel emotionally unstable lead to negative attitudes toward attending school, but they can also lead to increased overall stress in the child's life. The benefits of a high-quality early education environment with a qualified teacher can last years into a child's elementary and secondary education (NIEER, 2021b); however, a stressful early education environment can have damaging effects on the child's development as a whole.

What the states need to avoid is the perception that state-funded preschool is a sub-par education. This perception not only can damage state and federal funding opportunities, but it can also create the illusion that early childhood education is not valuable to young children. We know that a high-school education is vital for students before they enter the workforce, but it may not be beneficial for a high-school student to be in a math class with thirty-six other students. Not every student would get the individualized attention needed, and with that many students, the teacher would have to deal with many behavior-management issues. The same dynamic applies in the early education setting; however, since pre-K is not mandatory, many school districts would simply drop an unsuccessful program instead of taking the time to set it up correctly. For the pre-K system to be valuable to the state and to the children and families, the state must make it a priority for the program to be successful, including by providing the necessary funding and resources.

PROVIDING DEVELOPMENTALLY APPROPRIATE PRACTICE

Once the state dedicates funding and resources to the project, the public school system should not attempt to turn pre-K into a second-grade classroom focused solely on academics. Young children learn through play and exploration, so forcing young children to spend large amounts of time sitting at a desk doing structured activities will often create an entirely different set of behavior problems (NAEYC, 2020). This scenario often arises when an elementary or secondary education teacher is hired to teach in a pre-K classroom without any specialized training on pre-K skills and child development milestones. Even though the educator may have a teacher's certificate with the state, she is not best suited to teach pre-K if she does not understand the developmental milestones of the young child. The pre-K program must be designed for three- and four-year-old students, not elementary school students.

OFFERING CHILD CARE WHEN FAMILIES NEED IT

Finally, one last challenge to consider when creating a universal pre-K system is thinking about the needs of the working families and families who do not operate on traditional work schedules. Three hours a day of universal pre-K can be more of a challenge than a benefit for a working family. If all the adult caregivers in the home work during the day, the child needs to be in the early education setting much longer than three hours. As discussed in chapter 5, if the family did enroll the child in a half-day state-funded program, then someone would have to transport the child to another program that would care for the child for the remainder of the workday, which can be stressful for both the child and the parents. It would be easier for the family to pay out-of-pocket for a private setting so that there is one consistent classroom placement.

This is when a mixed-delivery system can be so beneficial for the families. State-funded pre-K enrollment slots in a child-care program that is open from 7 a.m. to 6 p.m. will be much more beneficial to a working family. The child can still benefit from a high-quality early childhood classroom that can help him prepare for kindergarten, but the family members do not require multiple child-care arrangements to cover the length of the workday. Caregivers who work evenings and weekends struggle with this issue even more than families who work typical office hours. If a parent works second or third shift, safe and healthy care for their children while they are at work is essential.

This is why family child-care homes need to be part of each state's mixed-delivery system. Not only can the child-care provider offer a quality early childhood education, but family child-care homes are also much more likely to tailor their hours of operation to the needs of the families who enroll. Home-based child-care providers may be available to care for the children on weekends or provide a nurturing sleeping environment at night while the parent is working. Also, some families simply want the option to choose the type of early care and education they want for their children. If the only option for pre-K is half-day preschool in the public school system, it does not meet the needs of all the families, and the state may be investing in a system in which families do not want to participate. Offering different types of early childhood education classrooms with a variety of locations, hours of operations, sizes, curriculums, and even cultural backgrounds allows families to choose the type of care that meets their needs.

Although there are many challenges to consider when designing a universal pre-K program within a state, it is still possible for states to create a universal pre-K system that can be successful and support thousands of families. It is critical to learn from the states that have successfully administered mixed-delivery early childhood systems and expanded to universal pre-K programs. Again, states must decide that early childhood education is a priority, but once they have, they have the potential to put together a program that can benefit children and families for years!

CHAPTER 9

Special Education and Mixed Delivery

As discussed earlier in this book, one of the many benefits of a mixed-delivery care system is that it provides resources and support for children with disabilities and their families. In this chapter, we will look at how federal and state laws protecting and helping people with special needs affects partnerships between private child-care providers and state and federally funded programs.

Most private child-care programs receive little or no state or federal funding. When a private business enters a partnership with a state or federal organization and receives public funding, it becomes responsible for implementing those funds with the integrity and accountability that state and federal laws surrounding those funds require. For private child-care programs, some of these state and federal requirements may already be in place simply to maintain a license to operate the program. For example, in order to receive a license from the state to open a child-care program, the program will already have to participate in the National Background Check Program mandated by the federal government. All the minimum child-care licensing requirements mandated by the state will have to be met simply for the program to open its doors. Those requirements must be met even if public funding is not available for the child-care program.

Once a private child-care program begins a partnership with a public program (state-funded preschool or Head Start), those public funds allow the child-care program to offer even more services to the children and families enrolled in the program. One of those services includes referrals for children with disabilities. This does not mean that the child-care program offers special education services; however, once the child-care program is a partner with a state or federal child-care service, then it has an obligation to ensure that families are guided through the special education process. In order for this to happen effectively, employees at a private child-care program must understand the laws surrounding special education and how they need to assist families through the referral process. These laws can also be important for child-care programs to apply in regard to their staff members.

AMERICANS WITH DISABILITIES ACT

The purpose of the Americans with Disabilities Act (ADA) is to make sure that children and adults are not a target for discrimination simply because they have a disability. This act looks at discrimination against individuals with disabilities that could be associated with employment, transportation, public accommodations, and access to state and federal government resources (US Department of Labor, 2022). This act is a civil rights law that protects the rights of a specific population of individuals. Title II of the ADA specifically looks at preventing the state and local governments from discriminating against individuals with disabilities. This is the portion of the ADA that the Department of Education helps to protect, specifically the portion that refers to the public school system and the higher education system.

Instead of providing actual education services to children with disabilities (which is addressed in a separate law), the Americans with Disabilities Act focuses more on giving children and adult access to all the same opportunities as typically developing individuals (US Department of Labor, 2022). For example, the act will focus on making sure that every building is accessible to individuals with disabilities by mandating wheelchair ramps and accessible elevators. The act is purposely a little vague because it is hard to envision every scenario in which an individual with a disability may not be offered the same opportunities as a typically developing individual, but the categories, such as transportation and employment, are listed to give guidance and make sure that essential life services are accessible to everyone.

A child-care program may also need to take into consideration the accommodations needed by an employee with a disability. Some responsibility is placed on the employee to disclose to the employer what her disability is and what accommodations are necessary in order for her to complete the job effectively. This open communication is especially necessary when an employee has an invisible disability (for example, epilepsy). It may be more obvious when an individual has a physical disability that the employer can see, and the employer understands that structural accommodations are needed.

INDIVIDUALS WITH DISABILITIES EDUCATION ACT

The Individuals with Disabilities Education Act (IDEA) is a law that ensures a Free and Appropriate Public Education (FAPE) for all students in the public school system (US Department of Education, 2019). Part B of the law speaks about children between the ages of three and twenty-one years of age, and Part C speaks about children between the ages of birth and thirty-six months of age. Part C focuses on giving infants and toddlers the necessary therapy supports in their natural environments, which they need if they have qualified for services. But Part B focuses on offering special education supports while enrolled in the public school system. There is also a transition process discussed for when children transition from Part C to Part B.

Unlike the ADA, IDEA is not a civil rights law. This law specifically focuses on education. It requires public schools to develop an individualized education plan (IEP) for eligible students with disabilities, outlining their educational goals, services, and accommodations necessary to support their learning. Although the IDEA lists disabilities that it works to support and protect, it does not guarantee each child an IEP simply because of a diagnosis. If the child's diagnosis does not affect his or her ability to learn and function in the classroom setting, then the child may not need an IEP. The child may only need some basic accommodations, and in that case, the child may be referred for a 504 plan instead of an IEP.

When a child qualifies for special education services, then the child will have an IEP, a legal document that ensures the public school system will offer the special education supports listed in the plan. If the child is under the age of thirty-six months, then the child will be issued an Individual Family Service Plan (IFSP) instead of an IEP. This plan focuses more on including the whole family in the child's developmental outcomes. Unlike a 504, the IEP or IFSP is much more structured. The plan will include the child's strengths, the family's concerns about the child's development and her ability to learn in the classroom setting, the results of the most recent evaluation, and the academic, developmental, and functional needs of the child (US Department of Education, 2019).

THE DIFFERENCE BETWEEN A 504 PLAN AND AN IEP

Not every child with a disability needs specialized instruction. An IEP details any specialized instruction that a child with a disability must receive. A 504 plan describes the accessibility requirements a child with a disability needs to have equal access to public education and services (University of Washington, 2022).

All members of the special education team (including the classroom teacher, the special education teacher, the diagnostician, the therapists, and the family) are allowed to give feedback on the final plan. Even though the family members are not education specialists, their suggestions on areas of concern and goals for the upcoming school year should be heard and valued. If the family members do not feel that the IEP addresses their concerns, they do not have to sign off on the document, and the family can appeal the decisions made in the special education meeting. The information recorded in the IEP is considered confidential according to the Family Education Rights and Privacy Act (FERPA), and any professional with access to that information (diagnosis, treatment, and student records) must use professional confidentiality (US Department of Education, 2019). This applies to both IDEA Parts B and C. Parents have the right to access their child's records upon request.

LEGAL DISPUTES

If family members do not agree with the decisions made regarding the child's access to special education services or with the decisions outlined in the IEP, then they have the right to a due process hearing (US Department of Education, 2019). This hearing would feel similar to a court case, and it is focused solely on whether or not the child is receiving a free and appropriate public education (FAPE). The family can disagree with the results of the evaluation, the diagnosis, the classroom placement, or with the implementation of services. For example, the child may have an IEP that awards the child certain services, but documentation shows that the child is not receiving those services. The family can then request a due process hearing to allege that the school is in breach of the IEP document because the required services are not being provided. This type of dispute is focused on the public school system, but if a child-care program or Head Start program are part of a mixed-delivery system, they may be asked to participate in the hearing.

IDEA AND PRIVATE CHILD-CARE PROGRAMS

IDEA is a law that was created for the public school system, but in a mixed-delivery framework it can affect private child-care programs. If the private child-care program is receiving a set amount of funding per child to enroll children in their program, then the program becomes a subcontractor of the public school system and will be responsible for meeting the education requirements of the IDEA funding. In most contractual settings, the private child-care program will refer the child to the contracting public school system for evaluation, diagnosis, and creation of an IEP or an IFSP. The public school system will either move the child to a classroom in one of the public school facilities or send the necessary therapists to the private child-care program to meet the requirements listed in the IEP.

If the child stays in the classroom at their child-care program, then that program will have a role in the child's special education needs. First, the family of the child will have to give permission for the child-care program to have access to the child's private educational information in the IEP. This can be a complicated process because technically, the child is being served in the classroom at the child-care program, so the child-care providers are the child's teachers. Despite that distinction, the IEP is still a contract between the family and the public school system.

The family must give consent to share that information with the subcontractor in order for the child-care program to review the IEP. Of course, it is in the best interest of the child for the early educators at the child-care program to understand the child's diagnosis and developmental goals, but the family has every right to be protective of that information. The family members may not want to share the IEP to prevent any bias against the child or have the child permanently labeled. If and when the family gives consent, then the child-care program can prepare to meet the child's needs in the classroom setting.

The teachers will need to be trained in how to implement the obligations of the IEP (or IFSP) and how to collect the required data to see if the child is making progress to meet her goals. The teachers and administrator will also have to follow the confidentiality requirements of the Federal Education Rights and Privacy Act. Only teachers that need information about the child's development and behavior should have access to the records, and this type of information should never be shared with other families. In some cases, the IEP will document that the child should receive a certain amount of time each week with a developmental interventionist or in cognitive support therapy. In preschool, that often counts as the time that the child works with a certified early childhood special education teacher (depending on the state's licensure requirements). If the classroom teacher in the child-care program is a licensed early childhood special educator, then she may be part of the list of therapists. If the teacher is not licensed or certified, then the public school may be responsible for sending a different specialist to work with the child for that amount of time. The school system may not be accustomed to sending a specialist for that requirement since most of the preschool teachers in the public school system would automatically fill that requirement. The child-care program should make sure that it is not responsible for filling that requirement if it does not have the qualified staff members to meet the obligation.

The best way for a private child-care program to be prepared for the obligations associated with providing care to children with disabilities in a mixed-delivery setting is to ask the school system to provide the program with training on special education preschool as soon as they enter into a partnership. The school system may decide to have all preschool students with an IEP served within the public school preschool classrooms. In that case, the child-care program would only need to be aware of supporting the family through the referral process. If children with disabilities will remain in the private child-care classrooms, then it is essential for the child-care program to understand its role. In that case, it is critical to understand from the beginning what the expectations from the public school system are in order to meet the requirements of all special education laws. This strategy will protect the children as well as the child-care program. Consider Jada's story.

> Jada is three years old and was diagnosed with Down syndrome prior to birth. Due to her diagnosis, she receives weekly speech therapy, occupational therapy, and physical therapy. She also sees a pediatric cardiologist due to a heart condition associated with Down syndrome. Since Jada has a diagnosed disability, she qualifies for an IEP with the public school system. The school district can provide all three types of therapy during the school day and monitor Jada's progress to make sure that she is achieving new developmental goals. The local elementary schools in Jada's district that offer public school preschool have only half-day classes, but Jada's mother and father both work full-time. Her local school district also has mixed-delivery classrooms in private child-care programs that are open for a full day. Since Jada's parents need full-time child care, the school district arranged for Jada to be enrolled in one of the partner child-care programs.
>
> Jada's child-care program is open from 7 a.m. until 6 p.m. Mondays through Fridays. It is also open on school holidays such as spring break and during the summer, so Jada can consistently stay at the same program with the same teachers. To partner with the public school system, the child-care program must have a teacher for the preschool program who meets the educational requirements of the public school preschool classroom. That is a larger expense for the child-care program, but in return, the center receives professional development training for its teachers, special education assistance, and a per-child stipend amount for each child who takes a partnership enrollment place. The therapists come to Jada's child-care program and work with her in the classroom on her therapy goals. They also train the teachers on the best ways to help Jada in the classroom. The techniques that the therapists are training the teachers to use are a benefit to all the children in the classroom.

Because Jada is technically enrolled through the public school system, even though she attends a private child-care program, her family does not have to pay tuition during the school year. When the school year ends for the summer, then the family is responsible for paying tuition if Jada continues to attend the program. Her parents can save up for those three months during the course of the school year to pay her summer fees, and they are grateful that Jada does not have to attend a different program where the teachers would have to be trained on how to work with their daughter. The continuity in care has been great for Jada, and since the teachers get so much support for the public school system during the school year, they have not been nervous about meeting Jada's needs.

CHAPTER 10

Professional Development in a Mixed-Delivery Early Education System

One of the most complicated aspects of a mixed-delivery early education system is to make sure that all children receive a commensurate education, regardless of which setting they choose to attend. The predominant reason for the differences in educational quality is the training and education experience of the teachers across settings. At a family child-care home, you might have a primary child-care provider who has had twenty years of experience but no formal education or training in early childhood. On the other end of the spectrum, the director of an early childhood program may be affiliated with a large university, have a master's degree in early childhood education, and be working toward her PhD. When teachers and assistant teachers receive continued training and professional development, it is much more likely that increased training will allow children to have a higher-quality early childhood classroom experience. This does not necessarily mean that teachers need additional training on the same lesson plans, but that all early childhood educators need training on appropriate learning environments, adult-child interactions, social and emotional development, and supporting children with challenging behaviors. In this chapter, we'll take a look at how to tackle this complicated issue by looking first at what professional development means in this field.

PROFESSIONAL DEVELOPMENT FOR EARLY CHILDHOOD EDUCATORS

To understand how professional development assists early childhood educators, we need to know how *professional development* is defined in this field. For early childhood education, profession development entails:

- continuous learning in the field of early education, child development, and special education.
- training workshops, conferences, in-service days, or higher education.
- hands-on training such as coaching and mentoring.

Within the framework of a mixed-delivery system, it is important for every educator to receive high-quality training so that one option in the mixed-delivery system is not noticeably better than another. A wide variety of organizations and individuals offer trainings and workshops. Some of that training is high quality, but not all those who advertise themselves as early childhood trainers or specialists promote correct practices. With that in mind, educators and administrators should consider several key factors for early childhood professional development:

- Quality training should be based on trusted developmental theories, proven research, and data collected from organizations that specialize in early childhood policy and practice.
- It is key to avoid early childhood training that is based on elementary education practices. Early childhood training should be developmentally appropriate for children younger than the age of five and should provide learning explorations through a play-based approach instead of sitting and listening to content.
- Training should include how to implement new teaching and behavior strategies effectively in the classroom.
- It is important for teachers and directors to consider this question when selecting training: "Will this training help me do my job better?"

Program administrators also have a key role in assisting staff members with participating in professional development training. The administrator should be in and out of the classrooms enough to assess the strengths and challenges of each staff member. With that knowledge, it is important for the administrator to help each staff member with an annual professional development plan. The plan should allow staff members to self-assess as well as receive feedback from the administrator. Once the administrator and the educator determine areas for growth, it is important to set professional goals that will help the teacher learn and grow in those areas. Staff members should be able to select short-term goals that could be addressed in under three months, but it is also important to have one or two long-term goals that the staff member can work on over time.

These established goals will help the director guide staff members toward the types of professional development that will help accomplish those goals. If a staff member has a goal to individualize classroom curriculum to the needs of each child, then the director may encourage that teacher to take trainings or attend a conference on emergent curriculum. Once the staff member attends the conference and collects a surplus of information, it is important for the director to create a program environment in which the teacher can come back and implement those changes in the classroom. There are several critical questions to consider:

- Does the teacher have the freedom to implement the changes learned during professional development?
- Is someone going to hold her accountable for implementing new skills once the program has invested in the teacher's professional development?
- Can the teacher evaluate her own performance in implementing new classroom techniques?

Aside from helping a teacher select professional development training, the director has other responsibilities. If the teachers want training on new skills that will benefit the children and families in the child-care program, it is important for the administrator to budget funds to pay for the cost of training and any essential resources that may be needed to accompany the training. The administrator can be a better guide for the teachers about professional development if she stays involved with professional organizations in the field of early education. This could be through national organizations such as the National Association for the Education of Young Children (NAEYC), Zero to Three, or Child Care Aware of America. Connections with these national groups can help the director stay connected to new teaching trends or data associated with successful education pilots.

Connections with local early childhood organizations can also be helpful for the child-care program. If the administrator participates in local peer learning groups or advocacy organizations, she is more likely to know about local resources for families or teachers. These connections can also allow administrators to find similar schools that may mentor teachers and to which newer teachers in the field can go to observe and see other educators implementing developmentally appropriate strategies in their own classrooms. Also, as an administrator continues her own professional development, it is more likely that she can be a better mentor for the teachers on staff in the child-care program.

When administrators place an obvious value on continuing professional development for all staff members, that priority inevitably benefits the staff members. Teachers feel more prepared and less stressed when they are well trained for their positions. Teachers also feel supported by the director when they develop a plan together and the director commits to assisting the teachers—and follows through on that commitment. Then, staff have the added benefit of learning new skills in the process. When child-care programs partner with state-funded preschool or Head Start programs, they can have access to a great deal more professional development, including trainers that specialize in special education, mental health, diversity and equity, and family partnerships.

COACHING AND MENTORING

Of course, it is important for administrators to remember that not all staff members are at the same point in their careers, so their professional development needs can differ also. New staff members may simply be trying to survive from day to day since the job can initially seem overwhelming. Their training may need to focus on basic child development principles and classroom management strategies. More experienced staff members may need someone to assess their performance in the classroom and give them feedback on how to improve and refine more specific skills. Both styles of training may be better administered through mentoring and coaching.

Coaching and mentoring are based on hands-on observation in the classroom setting. The coach or mentor watches the teacher in action and provides direct feedback on how the teacher can improve his existing skills. It is hard for a mentor to walk into a classroom and observe everything at once—lesson plans, classroom management, child interactions, classroom design, and so on. Instead, this style of professional development is most effective when a mentor and teacher first sit down together to talk about the teacher's goals for improvement. The mentor can provide upfront feedback on strategies to support that goal. The teacher can begin to practice the mentor's suggestions, and then the mentor can observe several times in the classroom over a designated time frame to see if the teacher is progressing toward the goal. Once the mentor and teacher feel that the goal has been completed, they can select another goal and use the same process.

Another example of a coaching and mentoring relationship is an apprenticeship. The registered apprenticeship program is run through the US Department of Labor (2022). The apprenticeship program offers options for students and adults who want to learn in a specific career field. A registered apprenticeship is a paid position in which the apprentice is new to working in the field of early childhood education. A mentoring teacher will assist in the apprentice's training to help guide her through the extensive number of mandatory teaching and technical assistance hours required by the program. The apprentice will also receive classroom training hours to help prepare her for working in the field of early education. Upon completing the apprenticeship program, the new teacher will receive a credential that is acknowledged in all states. The benefit of this type of training program compared to a different type of higher education program is the large number of hours of training offered in the classroom by the mentor teacher, along with the opportunity for the apprentice to be a paid staff member during the training.

CREATING A UNIFYING FRAMEWORK

As we have seen, a mixed-delivery care system can truly enhance the training, coaching, and mentoring opportunities for private child-care educators. However, the greater issue in training early childhood educators is its framework, or rather, its lack of a unifying framework. In early childhood education, each training program is slightly different than the next. Even a college degree in early childhood education can vary from college to college. This is the same for all education programs, including the K–12 system. All the educators may have a degree or license in their field, but depending on the college or the state, their training may not be consistent. If the education community looked at other career fields, such as nursing, it could possibly see a way to become more uniform.

Nurses earn specific degrees and degree levels, such as Certified Nursing Assistant (CNA), Associate's Degree in Nursing (ADN), and the Bachelor's Degree in Nursing (BDN). Both the ADN and the BDN lead to the student becoming a Registered Nurse (RN). These programs allow certifications to transfer from state to state much more easily than a teacher's license; furthermore, professional medical organizations require the curriculum to be more aligned so that nurses have the same required skill sets across the field, whether the nurses work in hospitals, private practices, clinics, nursing homes, or in school settings. Because of the education level, work experience, and job responsibilities of each nurse, there is a more uniform pay scale, and a nurse would never be paid less to work in pediatrics than to work with adults. This is the type of system that the early education field needs to consider for mixed-delivery classrooms.

POWER TO THE PROFESSION

In January 2017, a group of representatives from fifteen professional organizations representing early care and education for children from birth to age eight began meeting to discuss ways to further professionalize the field (Thornton et al., 2020). After a series of meetings to look at the educational qualifications of staff, wages, content of training programs, and other important issues surrounding early childhood professionalism, the task force published a list of recommendations. Their final report included their vision for the field of early childhood education, and it also included methods of implementation to launch their "Power to the Profession" platform.

One of the primary recommendations was to develop three levels of designation for professionals in early education (Thornton et al., 2020): Early Childhood Educator I, II, and III. This designation would include a license based on:

- completing a recognized and/or accredited professional recognition program,
- completing field experience, and
- passing an assessment.

This process would require that the licensure exam be affordable for all candidates, use multiple methods of assessment, and not reinforce any specific gender, cultural, or ethnic stereotypes (Thornton et al., 2020).

The recommendations would allow for three primary pathways to the different educator designations (Thornton et al., 2020). Those pathways would include:

- early childhood education certification/credential.
- early childhood education associate's degree.
- early childhood education bachelor's degree/initial master's degree.

Eventually, opportunities would be developed for early childhood educators to receive a specialization for their designation, but first they would have to receive the general education content (Thornton et al., 2020). Professional organizations could create and administer the specializations. For example, the National Association for Family Child Care may want to create a specialization for early childhood educators who work in family child-care homes, or Zero to Three may want to create a specialization for infant and toddler teachers. Such designations would allow for additional training as teachers continue to grow and learn in the field, but they would also allow for a deeper dive into content areas for teachers who work in those specialty areas each day.

The Power to the Profession task force also recommended that, along with professional designations, early childhood educators receive professional compensation (Thornton et al., 2020). With all early childhood educators falling into one of the three designations based on training, field work, and a final assessment, the industry would have more alignment, like the nursing field. Employers could base their wages and benefits packages on the employee's professional designation, years of experience, and job responsibilities, the same way that many other industries develop their salary scales.

The main goal is for all early childhood educators to enjoy adequate salary and benefits (Thornton et al., 2020). Then, eventually, educators could also be awarded compensation increases based on moving up their professional designation or as they accumulate additional years of experience. Compensation should not be based on the age of the children in their classrooms. Also, early educators in family child-care homes must learn to plan their salary into their budget so that they, too, are paid a competitive wage. If early childhood educators know they will receive adequate compensation, the industry will be much more likely to retain high-quality teachers. With more high-quality teachers, it is more likely that early childhood classrooms can maintain quality across a mixed-delivery setting.

IMPLICATIONS FOR STAKEHOLDERS IN THE MIXED-DELIVERY CARE SYSTEM

The implementation of these recommendations will definitely be complicated, and many different individuals and organizations will need to contribute to bring the plan to fruition (Thornton et al., 2020). First, professional training programs, both in universities and in non-college settings, will need to align their curricula so that students can graduate with proficiency in a set group of professional standards and competencies. Those standards and competencies will be the basis of the licensure exam so that students can obtain their professional designation. Each designation (I, II, and III) will have different levels of standards that must be maintained for the designations to be credible throughout the United States.

Child-care program owners and administrators play an important role in the implementation process because the private sector must begin to pay more for qualified educators in order to raise the professionalism of the field and attract the necessary workforce for private child-care programs to remain open (Thornton et al., 2020). Professional organizations will also be key partners in the implementation. Not only will professional organizations be responsible for the specializations to the Early Childhood Educator designation, but they will also need to join together to endorse this system to owners, parents, and state and federal officials for the system to be successfully implemented. Policy changes are not made without proof that they will benefit multiple groups of people. The professional organizations need to draft their message to show that educators, owners of child-care programs, families, and communities can all benefit from the proposed changes.

State and federal administrations also need to show their support through additional funding streams (Thornton et al., 2020). To compensate teachers with a reasonable salary and benefits package, child-care programs will need more funding. A mixed-delivery system will give private child-care programs some additional levels of funding, but additional funds will be needed to create pay equity across all mixed-delivery settings. That means that additional state and federal funding dollars will have to be used to support child-care programs and create an aligned system under which every child in an early childhood education system has access to a trained professional educator who is able to prepare the child to succeed when entering kindergarten.

As the mixed-delivery system spreads across states, high-quality teachers will continue to be a topic of conversation, particularly with the current workforce shortages across the country. A nationwide early childhood educator training program is not going to emerge overnight, but states and communities can begin to look at the model that Power to the Profession created as a baseline for making sure that children have access to equitable child care (Thornton et al., 2020).

CHAPTER 11

Pay Parity for Early Educators and How Mixed-Delivery Can Help

One of the greatest challenges for the field of early childhood education—whether we are talking about private child-care programs, federally and state-funded programs, or mixed-delivery early childhood systems—is the low level of compensation offered to early childhood professionals. Preschool teachers do not receive the same compensation that kindergarten teachers receive. Infant and toddler teachers do not receive the same amount of compensation that preschool teachers receive. The younger the age of the child, the lower the level of compensation. Regardless of the age range of the children, most child-care providers do not receive a competitive salary, and many are starting to leave the field due to this problem.

COMPENSATION IS THE PROBLEM

When you sit down to analyze the facts about compensation for early childhood educators, the information is abysmal.

- One in four child-care providers has at least one additional job in order to pay their bills (Fisher, 2021).
- Forty percent of child-care providers say that their child-care position accounted for less than 40 percent of their total income (Fisher, 2021).

- In 2021, the national average center-based child-care salary was around $13.00 per hour, when kindergarten teachers made an average of $32.80 per hour (Herschander, 2022).
- Infant and toddler teachers averaged even lower wages in 2021 with $11.00 per hour (Herschander, 2022).
- Eighty-six percent of child-care providers make $15.00 per hour or less (Sharrock and Parkerson, 2020).
- Child-care providers rank in the second percentile of pay in all career fields, meaning that 98 percent of career fields make a higher wage. Kindergarten teachers are in the sixty-first percentile, a much higher rate of compensation (Dichter and LiBetti, 2021).
- Half of the child-care workforce relies on some type of public assistance (Sharrock and Parkerson, 2020).
- Only 15 percent of child-care providers nationwide have health insurance through their employers (Sharrock and Parkerson, 2020).
- Seventy-six percent of child-care providers have some type of professional credential, a post-secondary degree, or a certification in early childhood education, and they are still making minimal wages (Coffey, 2022).

These types of statistics do not encourage new employees to enter the field, and many employees who enjoy their position working with young children must leave the field to care for their own families. The

EQUITY IN THE EARLY CHILDHOOD WORKFORCE

The early childhood workforce is 97 percent women, and more than two out of every five women are women of color (Herschander, 2022). Although child-care providers already receive a low wage, in 2019 Black women made an average wage of $11.27 per hour in the child-care industry, which was 76 percent of the $14.78 per hour that white employees averaged (Coffey, 2022). It is hard to isolate exactly what circumstances cause a wage to be lower for one individual compared to another. It could include years of experience, education level, the age range of the children being cared for, the tuition rates of the program, or the government subsidy reimbursement rate. Despite those variables, a significant trend showed Black women earning less pay for doing the same job in the field of early childhood education. The root of many of these variables relates back to systemic racism. When child-care providers are making even less than the average low wage, it contributes to their own experience in the poverty cycle and the inability to break out of that cycle. Women of color have been caught in this cycle of poverty in the caregiving workplace for centuries.

field of early childhood education shows a significant workforce shortage, which is affecting other industries because the US child-care programs allow workers in other industries to go to work (Mueller and Sutton, 2023). However, it is not difficult to figure out why there is a workforce shortage in the child-care industry. It comes down to salary. If child-care providers must work at least one extra job to pay their bills or if they must apply for government assistance after working a full-time job, then the industry is not supporting its employees and the employees will eventually leave.

Overall, the salaries indicate that the education system does not value the education of its youngest, most vulnerable students in comparison to the older children. If children in the first five years of development were respected in comparison to the amount of brain development and overall growth that occurs during that time period, early educators would be compensated with the highest salaries instead of the lowest.

WHAT ARE THE CONSEQUENCES?

The consequences of paying low salaries and offering little to no professional benefits to child-care providers are that providers are leaving the field for other jobs or other industries. Child-care providers with credentials are leaving to go to Head Start or public school preschool classrooms where they receive higher salaries and paid benefits (Hogan, 2021). Other child-care providers are leaving to work in retail, hospitality, or even warehouse jobs simply because they can make more money, receive benefits, and get respect for a job well done. Since 2020, one in ten child-care providers has left the field (Herschander, 2022).

When child-care providers who have left the field have been questioned about their decision, they have provided the following responses (Frank et al., 2021):

- They took a great deal of professional development training to become more skilled at their profession.
- They worked hard to create a positive and loving learning environment for their students.
- They loved the children and families they worked with at their program.
- They could not financially support their own families.

Even if child-care providers adore their jobs, they will leave if they cannot support their own families with their salaries. Ultimately, the well-being of their own family members must come first.

WHAT IS THE SOLUTION?

Staffing challenges are getting worse across the field of early childhood education, and compensation is both the problem and the solution (Hogan, 2021). To retain high-quality staff in the child-care field, compensation must be increased. A mixed-delivery approach to early childhood education certainly does not solve the issue of compensation in itself, but it does provide an opportunity to systemically address the problem as discussed below.

There are several different ways to think about increasing compensation: raising wages; improving benefits; and offsetting the cost of other expenses for the child-care workforce, including child care for child-care providers and health insurance. The first and primary method of fixing the compensation problem for child-care providers in the United States is to increase wages.

RAISING WAGES

Setting a standard for wages throughout the field is one way to address inequities across age range, educational setting, and funding stream (Leonhardt, 2021). The standards should account for job role, years of experience, and education level. Once those three variables are factored into the funding equation, there should also be a method to reduce racial disparities in salaries. Currently, preschool teachers in the public school system are paid more than preschool teachers in the private sector, and preschool teachers are paid more than infant and toddler teachers. Those issues could be addressed by looking at the qualifications and responsibilities of the teachers instead of the age range of the children and the setting of the classroom.

As early as 2018, several states, including Alabama, Hawaii, New Jersey, Oklahoma, and Rhode Island, began work on this process (Dichter and LiBetti, 2021). These states established preschool parity across the mixed-delivery system so that preschool teachers in the private sector are making commensurate pay with teachers in a public school system. Those programs participating in the state's mixed-delivery system follow a pay scale like that of the public school system, based on years of experience and education level. Of course, private child-care programs that do not receive any state or federal funding have the opportunity to set their pay rates at whatever level they choose. They have to compete with the mixed-delivery pay scale to obtain high-quality staff members. General market principles may encourage the private sector to increase its pay scale simply to be competitive.

Other states have taken steps toward pay parity. In Illinois, the state government set a goal to make center-based child-care salaries comparable to the public school system for assistant teachers through administrators, but the scale does not include family child-care homes (Dichter and LiBetti, 2021). The Minnesota salary scale also requires pay parity for private child-care programs with the public school system in its mixed-delivery system, and it sets its minimum wage range at $15 per hour, increasing with education and experience. North Carolina bases its pay scale on three separate credentials: an associate's degree, a bachelor's degree, and teacher licensure. Rhode Island is one of the first states to specifically look at pay parity for infant and toddler teachers and also to make salaries for those teachers commensurate with those of the public school system. Washington chose to assign certain child-care positions in mixed-delivery programs to pay-equivalent positions in the public school system to align the salaries based on education, years of experience, and job responsibilities.

Some states with a set pay scale for early childhood educators have specific requirements for the program to receive the supplemental pay to assist child-care programs to pay their staff the higher rate (Dichter and LiBetti, 2021). These requirements may include the following:

- The program must be licensed and regulated through the state.
- The program must include a minimum percentage of families enrolled in subsidy.
- The program must participate in the state's QRIS.
- The state may directly administer the bonus funding to staff members, and not the child-care program, to ensure that staff receive the incentive.
- Bilingual staff members may receive an additional financial incentive.
- A minimum pay ceiling may be required to qualify for the financial bonus.
- Staff members may be required to have a minimum education level or be in pursuit of an educational credential.
- Staff members may be required to work with a particular population such as infants and toddlers or birth to five years.
- Educators may have to work a minimum of fifteen to twenty hours per week to qualify for the financial incentive.

Some child-care programs may use their apprenticeships or scholarship programs to make sure that early educators have appropriate training and receive financial incentives for educational gains (Hogan, 2021). This is actually a method that can be used to prepare child-care programs to partner with state-funded preschool in a mixed-delivery setting. Teachers would be preparing for the educational requirements of the partnerships, which would lead them to the increased pay rates. Early childhood apprenticeship programs are growing in popularity throughout the United

States. High school juniors and seniors can work in a child-care program under a mentor teacher for school credit and eventually can receive an official apprenticeship certificate. They can potentially graduate from high school with a CDA certificate as a part of the apprenticeship program and be workforce ready.

IMPROVING BENEFITS

Many of the states that have been able to establish a competitive salary scale have still not been able to find a way to implement commensurate benefits. Other child-care programs may be able to offer their staff members one benefit, such as paid time off, but they do not have the financial resources to provide health-care or retirement benefits to their employees. States need to consider how child-care programs can support staff members with benefits, including paid time off, health insurance, and retirement plans (Hogan, 2021). The large-scale goal would be for all child-care programs to increase access to benefits, but within the frame of mixed-delivery programs, some of the additional funding stream should be used for an employee benefits package.

Even in child-care programs that offer a small amount of paid time off, it may be difficult for staff members to take leave from work since the adult-to-child ratios must be maintained in each classroom. This can mean that staff members struggle to plan vacation time around one another or that many employees do not get to take time off during holiday seasons. One possible way to support employees who would like to make use of paid leave is to establish and grow substitute pools of early childhood educators within local communities (Hogan, 2021). Child-care programs and mixed-delivery partners could work together to help ensure that willing substitutes have the necessary requirements, such as professional development plans, appropriate background checks, and annual training hours, so that they are ready to provide assistance to programs whose staff members want to take a day off of work. Knowing that the workforce shortage has affected jobs like substitute teachers, programs may want to think of innovative ways to attract providers to this type of work, such as allowing substitutes to bring their young child with them to the child-care program on days that they work as long as the child has the required paperwork on file.

OFFERING CHILD-CARE ASSISTANCE

Another way to support child-care providers with an additional benefit is to provide categorical eligibility for the child-care subsidy program to all child-care program employees. Kentucky was the first state to implement this program for child-care providers (Kentucky Administrative Regulations, Division of Child Care, 2022). Within the Kentucky child-care regulations on child-care subsidy, a child-care provider can qualify for child-care assistance in the following circumstances.

If a provider works a minimum of twenty hours per week in a child-care program, regardless of the position in the program, the child can qualify for child-care subsidy regardless of the family's total income. The teacher cannot be directly responsible for the care of their own child. For example, the child would attend the same child-care program, but another adult must be the primary teacher or caregiver.

Most child-care staff members would then have the opportunity to go to work with their young child in the building and still receive a larger salary than if child-care expenses were deducted.

This program is also a benefit to the child-care program, since many programs have offered a staff discount in the past. With the categorical eligibility for child-care subsidy, the child-care program gets the full amount of tuition from the state subsidy program for the employee's child, and the employee gets to keep a larger portion of her paycheck. The program will also allow a child to attend a different child-care program than the parent. For example, if a parent works in an early education program for children under the age of kindergarten, then the employee's child could still receive subsidy for the elementary school after-school program as a benefit. This program is a way for the state to offer a benefit to the child-care provider with the understanding that the child-care program may not have the funding to do so.

SUBSIDIZING HEALTH CARE

Finally, child-care programs need to find ways to subsidize the cost of health care for their employees (Hogan, 2021). Working in the child-care field puts a staff member more at risk of catching contagious illnesses simply because the employees are in such close contact with young children. If an employee is continuously exposed to illness without the opportunity to see a doctor when they get sick, it is setting them up for a financial disaster once an illness progresses to the point that the employee must seek medical attention. It is also important to remember that many potential employees who work in child-care programs could need health insurance to care for chronic health conditions. Some teachers may need to turn down any position that does not offer a minimum amount of health insurance, so by not offering any health-care benefit, child-care programs may be losing an entire population of employees who could be wonderful assets to their programs.

Child-care programs do not have to be solely responsible for covering the cost of an employee's health insurance, but the ultimate goal is to find a way to offer an affordable health-care plan to everyone who works a full-time position in the facility. In a mixed-delivery child-care program, it may be possible for the state-funded preschool or Head Start program to offer a health insurance option to their partner programs. Child-care programs need to explore lots of options, talk to insurance brokers, and find out what staff members do not have access to medical coverage through a parent, a partner, or a spouse.

If child-care programs can find an overall compensation package (salary and benefits) that can continue to increase over time with education and experience, then child-care providers are more likely to stay at the program and in the field that they love. Mixed-delivery programs have the added benefit of public funding (either from the state or the federal government) and should use this additional funding to support staff members. A high-quality child-care program requires high-quality staff members who are appreciated by their employers. Programs are more likely to be successful when the early childhood educators are well trained on child development principles, and the educators enjoy their positions more when parents and administrators treat them like true professionals.

CHAPTER 12

Planning and Implementing a Mixed-Delivery Early Childhood System

As we've explored in previous chapters, the benefits of a mixed-delivery early childhood education are great. However, communities must make a big jump from agreeing mixed delivery is a good idea to actually implementing it. This type of transition requires planning and should not be rushed. The planning process, with the necessary partners, can make the difference between a successful attempt at implementation and a failed effort. In this chapter, we will look at the steps cities and states should take to ensure a successful mixed-delivery system for early childhood education. To start, stakeholders need to assess the needs of the community, see who should be involved in the planning process, and then develop concrete strategies to make the system happen in a city or statewide capacity (Reed et al., 2019). These steps include the following:

- Determining the need for partnerships
- Identifying the stakeholders who need to be at the table
- Establishing how the stakeholders meet and communicate
- Creating the vision of the partnership
- Developing data-driven strategic goals
- Creating a formal partnership agreement

DETERMINING THE NEED FOR PARTNERSHIPS

Before embarking on the long journey of implementing a citywide or statewide mixed-delivery preschool system, stakeholders should start by assessing the need for mixed-delivery preschool in the immediate area (Reed et al., 2019). The advisory team can ask the following questions:

- Are the child-care programs in the area financially unstable? Has there been an increase in child-care program closures?
- Are children who qualify for publicly funded early education (Head Start or state-funded pre-K) not enrolling because of the hours of operation or the school-year calendar?
- Is quality early childhood education accessible for all families, or is there a population of families who do not have access to quality care?
- Is there a state regulation or law that mandates a certain percentage of child-care partnerships?
- Are there child-care programs that need funding and resources to maintain higher quality?
- Are child-care programs in the area willing to partner with publicly funded programs?
- Do child-care programs need more support with assessment and services for children with disabilities?

The answers to these initial questions will determine if child-care programs need the public-private partnerships to help stabilize their funding, if the current state-funded preschool model is serving all the children who need support, and if the two entities are willing to begin the partnership process. If recent laws mandate a percent of mixed-delivery preschool opportunities, then the community obviously needs to form those partnerships; but if the partners enter into these agreements unwillingly, then the advisory team may need to work on ways to develop and strengthen relationships to be successful moving forward, even though the partners may be hesitant.

IDENTIFYING THE STAKEHOLDERS THAT NEED TO BE AT THE TABLE

Once a state or city identifies the need for mixed-delivery preschool, it is essential to determine which stakeholders need to be invited to the table to assist with planning and make sure that children, families, child-care programs, public early education systems, and the business community all benefit from the new system (Reed et al., 2019). Depending on the community and the infrastructure that is already in place, potential stakeholders could include:

- Head Start grantees
- Public school system—preschool coordinator, the superintendent, and so on
- Child-care resource and referral agency—recruitment of child-care programs
- Families and caregivers
- Financial investors
- State policy makers—legislative or executive branch
- Early childhood community partners—advocates and philanthropists
- Experts from visiting states and communities with mixed-delivery preschool
- Members of the business community—manufacturers, hospitals, retailers—all with vested interest in consistent child care for employees

It is also important to determine whether one planning team will do all the planning for the whole state, or if there will be regional listening sessions to allow local concerns to be expressed. This could mean that one advisory council is created at the state level, but the state advisory council travels to local communities where a sub-committee with local leadership expresses the concerns of their community. This would give the state advisory team the opportunity to see if each community has the same concerns. For example, if the state is using a market-rate survey to set the child-care subsidy costs across the state, then the advisory team may hear that child-care programs in rural, low-cost-of-living states have lower quality programs due to a lower subsidy reimbursement rate. These rural communities may need to partner with a state-funded preschool or Head Start program just to increase their quality level since they have even fewer resources than in urban areas.

An effort to hear the concerns of the different regions can also help a state advisory group identify areas that:

- have more child-care deserts.
- have little to no infant or toddler care.
- have little to no after-school care for elementary students.
- are not able to pay staff members a living wage.

- have a higher rate of staff shortages.
- have more families who qualify for Head Start or state-funded pre-K due to income eligibility.

Making sure that all members of the stakeholder team can see a full picture of the state's or city's needs will allow them to make the best decisions possible for the state or city as a whole.

ESTABLISHING HOW THE STAKEHOLDERS MEET AND COMMUNICATE

Every state or city in our nation has an excessive number of task forces that schedule regular meetings, and some may see little or no progress on their efforts over a considerable period of time. To make sure that this advisory board creates a viable plan for the implementation of a successful mixed-delivery preschool program, the advisory group determines when and how they are meeting and how they will share the information they bring back to the group (Reed et al., 2019). To create a plan based on data-informed decisions, the members of the team may need to do a fair amount of reading and research between meetings (ideally, one member is in charge of disbursing the reading materials to make sure that all team members receive the information). To ensure that each sector is represented in the decision-making process, the team's leadership should set meeting times when all committee members are most likely to attend. If the committee has a set amount of time to make recommendations on the set-up of the state's system, such as a six-month window, then the committee may need to meet more than once per month to review all the collected information and discuss what the best option for the state is.

The committee will also need to determine the best set-up for meetings. If committee members are located all over the state, it may be more efficient to have virtual meetings; however, if meetings are designed to be longer meetings with informational presentations and brainstorming sessions, then it may be beneficial for committee members to dedicate the time to attend in-person meetings. The committee members will also need to consider if they will have non-traditional meetings, such as touring child-care programs that are mixed-delivery partnerships. If the committee invites out-of-area partners to make presentations on how they have implemented mixed-delivery partnerships in their own states or cities, then the meetings may need to be determined at the convenience of the visiting state's presenters. Also, it is important to establish a reliable communication system to make sure that all members are receiving important updates. These efficiencies will make sure that all voting members have necessary information and can make key decisions.

CREATING THE VISION OF THE PARTNERSHIP

Creating a joint vision for the mixed-delivery system is really the foundation of the advisory council (Reed et al., 2019). If each member sees the mixed-delivery system as serving a different purpose, then it will be hard to determine policy and funding priorities. Advisory board members must ask themselves a lot of questions about the purpose of the system and why the state or city needs the system in place, which may include the following:

- What does the state need?
- What does the state hope to gain from implementing a mixed-delivery program?
- What is the purpose of the mixed-delivery structure for the state?
- How will the state contribute to the program?
- Is the framework sustainable in this state?
- Which children and families is the state hoping to assist?
- What will families and children gain from implementing a program like this?
- What will child-care programs and the public school system need to implement a program like this?
- How can all the organizations involved in this program work together to benefit the children and families?
- What is the vision statement of the mixed-delivery program for the state?

The board members should start their advisory committee meetings by establishing this vision with a focus on whom the program is for and what goals they want to see emerge from the program. Once the vision is established, then all further decisions about the program should relate back to the vision. If the vision is focused on supporting low-income families and children at risk of falling behind developmentally, then the program needs to be set up to focus on those children. It does not mean that the vision cannot change several years down the road, but the initial vision statement should be the guiding star for the program's development.

This also means that if the state has a secondary focus besides simply providing quality education, such as allowing all families to participate in the workforce and developing a strong economic foundation in the state, then that focus also needs to be included in the vision statement. A vison statement is not as long as a mission statement. It should be succinct, free from jargon, and comprised of two or three sentences. At the same time, a vision statement can be a lofty aspiration; it is meant to be idealistic and inspiring to everyone who reads it. If the vision is to provide universal pre-K to all students living in the state so they can be prepared for kindergarten, that goal will not be implemented quickly, but it succinctly describes the vision for the program. The vision statement should also include what makes this project different from any other project on which the state is working. For example, many organizations in the state are working on providing child care to working families, in the private sector or through state-funded projects. The vision statement for a mixed-delivery program can stand out by stating that all four-year-old children will qualify for free early childhood education in a variety of different settings that the family can select from to make the best choice for their individual situation. It is also important not to make the vision statement time limited, because a project of this scope can take a government agency a fair amount of time to organize and implement.

DEVELOPING DATA-DRIVEN STRATEGIC GOALS

When the state or city is planning to invest a large amount of funding into a project like mixed-delivery child care, the plan needs to be based on data from reliable sources that not only shows the need for the program but also high success rates for similar implementation plans (Reed et al., 2019). In the research community, that typically means collecting data from university-based research, state systems, or national think tanks and research facilities that focus on the specialty area. Once the data is collected, the committee members need to appoint a member to aggregate the data and offer a presentation on the trends. Alternatively, each member needs to spend time reviewing the data to make sure they understand what it says. Decisions made in the advisory group should be based on the data, even if the state needs to adapt its mixed-delivery plan to be slightly different than other states due to regional needs.

Data can also be used to set goals and prioritize which goals should be met first. Case studies of other states should show the building blocks of how states established their systems, for example, establishing an advisory council with multiple stakeholders before rewriting state policy. These previous building blocks can help a state establish a timeline for priorities, which may look like the following:

- Assemble a state stakeholder group.
- Create a vision statement.
- Draft new child-care and state-funded preschool regulations.
- Create a training webinar for state partners before roll-out of new regulations.

The top priority would be to assemble the stakeholder group that will create the vision statement and draft new regulatory requirements, since later steps in the process will depend on that first step. However, each step will still be based on data-informed decisions. For example, who should be in the stakeholder group? The stakeholder group can be assembled for organizations that consistently contribute to open comment on early childhood processes within the state. The appointing authority can also look at other states that have assembled this type of group and see which stakeholders successfully contributed to their advisory councils. Well-informed decisions will help the committee's plan be more stable in the long-term and will give the committee a solid foundation when they must defend their recommendations for a legislative committee, town council, or a government contract review board.

CREATING A FORMAL PARTNERSHIP AGREEMENT

The final step in the planning process is to begin implementing formal partnership agreements between the administering organizations (Reed et al., 2019). If the department of child care and the department of education are to be the primary organizations that will administer the program at the state level, they may need to enter into a memorandum of agreement (MOA) to share essential data between the two agencies. At the local level, school districts and Head Starts that partner with child-care programs will need to determine a set of outcomes and requirements that are attached to the funding streams. When contracts or MOAs are implemented, the contributing organizations also must consider what would occur to funding or data sources in case of a breach of contract. Contracts should be written and supervised by a practicing attorney, but partnering organizations need to consider what requirements need to be included in the contract for the partnerships to work. (See chapter 13 for more information on contracts and legal partnerships.)

Once the planning process is complete, the different partners can sign the contracts, and organizations can begin to implement services with accountability procedures in place. If it appears that the planning process did not account for all the possible barriers to implementation, then the advisory team can come back together to redirect their goals and avoid future complications. After implementation, the advisory team should still continue to meet regularly (though not necessarily as frequently) to create a continuous improvement process in which the current system is evaluated and the committee continues to look for ways to improve the preschool system.

CHAPTER 13

Contracts and Legal Partnerships

Any time that a mixed-delivery partnership is created, the two (or three) organizations agree to share funding and meet the highest level of quality shared between the groups. This also means that an agreed-upon contract will be drawn up between the two organizations to detail the expected outcomes for both organizations. All contracts should be created by a licensed, practicing attorney to make sure that the contract is valid and executable. Although the lawyer will be the expert on how the contract is implemented and created, the partnering organizations need to ensure that certain areas of content are included in the contract to meet the financial and regulatory requirements of both organizations:

- Partner obligations
- Provider requirements
- Staff requirements
- Financial management
- Records, attendance, and confidentiality
- Performance evaluations
- Contract terms, renewability, and termination

However, the first step before creating a contract is to make sure that all parties involved work with the same understanding of key terms in the child-care field.

DEFINING KEY TERMS

First, the contract must be specific about the distinction between *full-day* and *part-day* education. Child-care programs often define *full-day care* as ten to twelve hours of operation, for example 6 a.m. to 6 p.m.; however, Early Head Start programs often categorize *full day* as six hours of care or longer. In the public school system, full-day care may be typical school hours, such as 7:45 a.m. to 2:45 p.m. That could also mean that a child in a full-day program may still need after-school child care until a parent is able to leave work and pick the child up.

Contracts also need to define what a *part-day* program entails. Most part-day public school and Head Start programs are three to four hours a day, but the state's child-care assistance program may define a part-time program as any care less than twenty-five hours per week. All these definitions must be concrete before any particular organization is required to offer a daily part-day or full-day program so that they fully understand their obligation.

Eligibility is another key term to define. Each type of program (private child care, Head Start, and state-funded preschool) has its own measures to determine eligibility. When the two programs blend, they may align their eligibility requirements, or they may have two separate categories for eligibility with different funding streams. For example, if a Head Start program and a child-care program form a partnership, the child-care program may agree to save twenty enrollment slots in its program for children who are eligible for Head Start. That means that the income of those families must be at or lower than 100 percent of the Federal Poverty Level (FPL). Those children would also be able to apply for the state's child-care subsidy system to provide the child-care program with blended income. The other children in the child-care program would have to follow the state's child-care subsidy guidelines for applying for tuition assistance. For example, if the state offers child-care subsidy for families at 200 percent of the Federal Poverty Level, then only families in that income bracket could apply. All other families would be responsible for tuition.

Aside from income, the partnering organizations may have other eligibility factors to consider. Children diagnosed with a disability may automatically qualify for a spot in state-funded preschool. In a state with universal pre-K, the only requirement may be the student's age. Other states may offer pre-K to any child who is four years old, but there may be a lottery to see which children are offered the spots. The contract must outline these eligibility requirements so that both organizations agree on which children will be served in the program.

Other key definitions are terms such as *teacher* or *assistant teacher*. Many programs use the term *teacher* to define any adult in the building who works with the children in the classroom, but contracts are typically not that broad. The main reason to differentiate is because *teacher* and *assistant teacher* typically have education and training requirements associated with them. The teacher may also have different job responsibilities such as planning the curriculum and supervising the assistant teacher.

Wrap-around services is another term that needs to be defined in contracts because it is not always used by all agencies. Head Start and Early Head Start provide a wide array of wrap-around services, including health services, family education, diapers, formula, and home visits. Health services may include immunizations, doctor's visits, vision assessments, dental visits, and transportation to and from these visits. State-funded preschool may offer some wrap-around services through the family resource centers, but the school system's definition is usually not as broad as Head Start programs. Private child-care programs do not receive any funding to offer these types of support.

When a private child-care program or a state-funded preschool program enters into a partnership with a Head Start program, it can be overwhelming at first to understand the full array of services that can be offered to the families enrolled in the program. The same definition is needed for private child-care programs entering a partnership with state-funded preschool. Although the school's family resource center or the Head Start's resource coordinators may still be in charge of offering these services, all partners need to understand what services are available to families and when to refer families for additional assistance.

Finally, partnering programs should define the difference between *excused* and *unexcused absences*. Many child-care subsidy programs allow a limited number of unexcused absences before a child is at risk of losing this service. State-funded preschool is typically not a mandatory program, but depending on each district's policies, a child may lose her enrollment due to excessive absences. Head Start programs also have their own way of tracking attendance. All children will miss school at times, due to illness or other unavoidable circumstances; however, if children have excessive absences, the child-care program will not provide the same benefits as if they attend on a regular basis.

PARTNER OBLIGATIONS

Once the partner organizations understand the terminology used in the contract, the next step is to outline essential obligations that are expected from the partner that is receiving funding to provide a service. These obligations range from how the funding is spent to how the program will maintain mandatory regulations. The partner distributing funds also needs to determine how it will evaluate the program that is receiving the funding.

It is essential for both partners to understand the regulations and policies they must meet to operate as a mixed-delivery program. If the partnership involves a private child-care program, then the program must meet the state's minimum child-care licensing requirements. In most cases, these will be the lowest set of standards that the program is responsible for meeting; however, there are occasions where one or two of the child-care regulations are more challenging than the Head Start or public school requirements. A mixed-delivery partnership means that the program is responsible for meeting the highest level of requirements between the two separate organizations. Administrators must try to learn all regulations. Also, if the program is asked to meet regional or national accreditation that is more challenging than the regulatory requirements, then the administration must also learn the rules of the accrediting body (such as the National Association for the Education of Young Children).

Once the program understands its obligations, it is clear how it will be evaluated. Many states use tools such as the *Early Childhood Environment Rating Scale*, third edition (Harms, Clifford, and Cryer, 2014) to rate their programs through the QRIS system. Head Start programs will use tools such as the Classroom Assessment Scoring System (McMillan, 2004) to evaluate Head Start or Early Head Start classrooms. Mixed-delivery programs that are being assessed with these tools will need to understand what they are expected to score on these tools as part of their contractual obligation. They may also be required to have a certain number of staff members trained in how to use the tool so that they understand the expectations.

Along with the assessment tools, mixed-delivery programs may undergo impromptu inspections by the partner that is providing the funding. The contract should include information about these inspections so that both partners understand that these visits do not have to be announced; that any policy violations found during the inspections will need to be addressed immediately; and that the partner providing the funding offers technical assistance to correct the policy violation if there is any confusion on why a protocol is not being implemented correctly.

The attorney writing the contract should consider what facility and maintenance requirements need to be in place. State child-care regulations, fire marshal requirements, and health department regulations require that the building be in a certain condition in order to be operational. In the event that the building has any type of damage or that essential appliances no longer work properly, it may be necessary to include a timeline for completing repairs. If the organization providing the funding is offering only a flat fee per year or per child, the lawyer may want to include language on which organization is responsible for paying for repairs.

These same types of details may need to be outlined for classroom materials, including furniture, playground equipment, and learning materials. The funder may initially provide items such as furniture or playground materials with the expectation that the other partner will maintain the materials in good condition for a certain amount of time. If the materials need to be replaced before that time, then the partner would be responsible for that cost. Regardless of who funds these types of purchases, the obligation should be listed in the contract so that the two organizations do not fight over who is responsible for the purchases at a later time during the contract period.

Insurance, particularly liability insurance, is essential in any contract. Some types of insurance are required in order to have a child-care license in certain states. Insurance for the building, particularly for weather damage, may be required before the facility is allowed to open and enroll children in the program. Liability insurance may also be required by the state. But even if it is not, a partnership program must make sure that each contractual partner is covered in the event of an emergency. This is especially important when it comes to situations where a child or a staff member is injured in the facility. The level of insurance and appropriate deductibles should be discussed with an insurance broker to make sure that the program is covered to match its needs. The part to remember is that there are liability issues involved when caring for other people's children, so liability insurance is important for a successful business, even if the state does not mandate it.

If the program offers transportation, which should also be detailed in the contract if it is expected, then automobile insurance will also be a requirement. Not all child-care programs offer transportation since the maintenance of the vehicle and the cost of the insurance can be a substantial expense. However, many Head Start programs and state-funded pre-K programs offer transportation, as it may be the only way that students can attend. That does not mean that a child-care program would be mandated to provide transportation, but it should be discussed in advance and detailed in the contract, specifically due to the additional costs. The program may only be expected to provide transportation for drop-off and pick-up, or there may be additional reasons for transportation such as field trips, medical appointments, and so on. The uses for transportation can also be included in the contract if needed.

STAFF REQUIREMENTS

The most valuable asset to any child-care program is its staff, and contracts need to detail what is expected of teaching staff and support staff. Some requirements will apply to anyone employed in the early education program, for example, a minimum age for anyone employed in the program and background checks for all staff. The National Background Check Program through the federal government is required in all licensed child-care and Head Start programs. Some state-funded preschool programs or individual organizations may impose additional requirements to ensure that the highest levels of security are maintained. The funding partner should detail all background check requirements in the contract. The providing partner may also want to detail how many staff members and which types of each category of staff it wants to fund so that additional hires will be funded by the partner organization.

Every early childhood education program has different categories of staff members, which can include the following:

- Lead teachers
- Assistant teachers
- Floating teachers
- Substitutes
- Administrators
- Food service staff
- Family service workers
- Bus drivers
- Volunteers

Contracts should outline the specific requirements for each of these positions, including the mandatory level of education for each position and previous experience, if applicable. Along with attaining a certain level of education, all early childhood education staff members must engage in ongoing training. Some organizations merely state a number of clock hours of training that staff need to complete. Other organizations create individualized professional development plans that explain in which areas the staff need further instruction and then hold staff members accountable for training in those areas. Contracts should outline how strict the organization will be about the type of training that each staff member completes as well as outline staff training that every staff member is mandated to take, such as the preservice training required by the federal government or specific trainings that all Head Start and Early Head Start programs must complete.

Along with the requirements placed on staff members, contracts should detail the obligations that the mixed-delivery programs must fulfill to support those staff members. The funding organization may have a mandated pay scale that they want to use to maintain pay parity with other similar programs that they administer. The organization providing the funding might establish base pay for certain types of positions and allow the program delivering the services more freedom to determine how far above the minimum they wish to pay to remain competitive in the field. Since Head Start programs and state-funded preschool programs often run on a ten-month school year, and child-care programs typically run on a twelve-month year, it is important to establish the duration of each contract. If a Head Start program provides only ten months of funding, but the child-care program with which they are partnering is open for a full twelve months, then the child-care program would be responsible for the additional two months of funding.

Another way that the mixed-delivery program may be required by contract to support its employees is with a benefits package such as medical insurance or paid time off for staff members. If a child-care program that has not previously offered benefits now partners with a Head Start program or a state-funded preschool, it may be required to offer staff members a benefits package. Adding insurance will require the child-care program to work with an insurance broker to add a benefits package. Adding paid time off and planning time will require the program to pay for additional staffing hours. All expectations and obligations should be explained to help the mixed-delivery program establish an accurate budget.

FINANCIAL MANAGEMENT

Making sure that funding is spent appropriately is one of the most important reasons for establishing a contract in any business partnership. Again, this portion of the contract should be established by a lawyer and accountant to make sure that it is beneficial and feasible for both partners. During the brainstorming discussion before the contract is finalized, the partner organizations should first establish whether the funding partner will pay the program a flat rate for its services or a per-child amount. Once that is decided, the contractual amount (including the funding schedule) needs to be detailed. The funder may provide the funding in one lump sum; however, it is most common to disperse a monthly payment divided up by a ten-month or twelve-month contract structure.

Once the provider organization knows the amount of funds it will be receiving, they must understand any requirements on how those funds are spent. For example, with federal Child Care and Development Block Grant (CCDBG) funds, the federal government tells each state a percentage breakdown. The largest percentage of the funds must be spent on direct services; however, the CCDBG funds also need to be spent on quality services and administrative fees. In a smaller partnership that involves one early education facility, it is more likely that the largest portion of funds would be spent on staffing. Other items that may factor into the contract could be professional development training, classroom materials, consumables such as daily meals and cleaning supplies, fixed expenses such as facility costs and insurance, or administrative expenses such as office supplies. The budget percentage breakdown needs to be detailed in advance and outlined in the contract.

Along with knowing how to spend the funding stream, the organization receiving the funding also needs to understand the accountability measures that will be expected of them to make sure that funds are spent correctly. Most funders will require some type of monthly financial report explaining how funds were spent. The funder will need to decide if they will require a certain type of report or if it will allow the organization to submit whatever type of monthly financial statement it already uses. The funder will also need to consider some type of auditing system, whether it is an annual planned audit or a surprise auditing system used as needed.

RECORDS, ATTENDANCE, AND CONFIDENTIALITY

Mixed-delivery programs must keep financial reports and plan audits on financial records; similarly, they must have the same type of system in place for enrollment and attendance records. State child-care systems, Head Start programs, and public school systems all have requirements for what types of records must be on file for children and staff members. Although many of the enrollment documents for the children will be the same for all programs, certain programs will have additional requirements, such as family income verification. The contract needs to explain that all children have up-to-date enrollment documents, and it needs to detail which documents are required. Staff documents need to follow the same type of procedure. The mixed-delivery program must maintain all required employment documentation for each staff member, and the contract must explain which documents are required.

Child enrollment documentation may include the following:

- Enrollment form with contact information for the child's legal guardians
- List of adults who can pick up the child from the program
- Release for emergency medical care
- Emergency contact information
- Immunization records
- Family income information for eligibility requirements
- Custody documentation
- Medical emergency plan (if needed)

Staff documentation may include the following:

- Name, address, phone number, and date of employment
- Completed National Background Check
- Proof of educational requirements
- Documented annual training hours
- Emergency contact information
- Immunization records and/or TB skin test results
- Doctor's statements stating staff member's ability to complete the job duties
- Annual performance evaluations

After each child has enrollment paperwork on file, the funder will also need proof of attendance. Some state subsidy systems require a handwritten signature from the guardians to verify the children's attendance. Other states may allow for a digital system of signing children in and out each day. Whatever type of system the funder requires, there must be a way to look at the children's overall attendance in the event of an audit. Particularly with federal funding sources, the program will need to verify each child whose enrollment is paid for with federal dollars is attending the program. The contract needs to document which type of system will be required so that the organization can maintain compliance with all attendance requirements.

When any early childhood education program begins collecting student and staff records, it gathers a great deal of personal information. The funding program needs to put procedures in place to make sure that personal information is not shared. The funder may want to detail which information should be designated as confidential and how confidential information should be stored. It also may be important to have all staff members trained in how to handle confidential documents.

PERFORMANCE EVALUATION

Each funder must find a method to evaluate the contract with the partnering organization. This may be a tool that the organization creates or a simple checklist of objectives. The partnering organization needs to understand the evaluation period, such as an annual or semi-annual evaluation. To ensure that the partnering organization is complying with the requirements of the contract, the lawyer may want to include a clause with a probationary period during which the organization can correct any deficiencies. The completion of the contract objectives can be a key component for the partnering organization to be considered for contract renewal.

CONTRACT TERMS, RENEWABILITY, AND TERMINATION

The contract should give clear details on the length of time for which it lasts. It should also explain to the partnering organization if the organization is eligible for contract renewal and if the contract renews automatically. Along with renewal information, the contract should explain which circumstances would allow for the contract to be broken and which parties are eligible to break the contract.

CHAPTER 14

Next Steps: Advocating for Mixed-Delivery Care

If a mixed-delivery early education system seems to be a possible solution to the child-care crisis, then each state or local city government must find a way to rally their communities to implement this new structure. As illustrated earlier in this book, some states have provided structurally sound examples of how the system can work, both for expanded mixed delivery and universal pre-K. With an understanding of how early education models work, other communities should be able to implement a system that works best for the local community. Prior to the implementation process, each community or state must start its campaign for why this system change is necessary, and that means advocacy at the state and local levels. The first step in this process is an education campaign.

CONDUCTING AN EDUCATION CAMPAIGN

The education campaign may be the largest step toward advocating for a mixed-delivery early childhood education system because many people do not understand what a mixed-delivery system looks like or how it would work in the community. To explain why it would benefit the children, the families, and the child-care programs involved, everyone has to understand how the system works. (They also must understand that mixed delivery does not mean universal pre-K, although it can be, and that it is rarely a mandatory process.)

The first step of the education campaign should be with child-care providers. They need to understand both what a mixed-delivery early education system is and how it can help the child-care community. If they misunderstand the mixed-delivery process, they might be hesitant to support it. If they feel such a system will compete against their business model or require them to change it completely, they might well oppose it. However, if they understand that participating in mixed delivery gives families more child-care options, along with infusing money into the private child-care sector, then they will be much more willing to participate.

Some child-care owners and advisory boards may be willing to sit down and hear an extended presentation, but the chances are that their time and attention are focused on operating their businesses. Advocates for mixed delivery may have only a short amount of time to start the conversation and catch the interest of the business operators. With that in mind, advocates should have talking points ready as soon as the discussion comes up, such as:

- A mixed-delivery system keeps child-care programs from having to compete with state-funded pre-K and Head Start programs.
- Mixed delivery would allow a child-care program to reach maximum enrollment with a steady funding source and would provide children and families with more resources than they are able to fund on their own, such as special education services or supports for families.
- All children in the child-care program will benefit from the mixed-delivery services, not just those who qualify for Head Start or state-funded preschool.
- A mixed-delivery system will still allow child-care programs to show their unique characteristics since the system is set-up to offer families more choices.

Of course, these examples do not include all the reasons that child-care programs can benefit from participating in a mixed-delivery child-care program, but they can help to ignite the interest of an owner who is ambivalent or was previously opposed to the idea of mixed-delivery preschool.

Once child-care programs begin to understand and show interest in participating in a mixed-delivery system, the next step is to show them how to use their voice to influence their state systems. Child-care providers are continually trained on how to work with young children, but many of them feel uncomfortable speaking to city and state government officials to ask for policy changes. Local trainings on the legislative process can help prepare them to advocate for themselves, their businesses, and the community-wide value of creating a mixed-delivery child-care system. These types of workshops can also be important to simply encourage child-care providers to speak up for themselves if they have never done so before. Elected officials are interested in hearing from small businesses in their communities because they were elected to represent their constituents. It is important for child-care providers to understand that they are the constituents that the legislative members want to hear from. Of course, all of these steps can also be done at the city level when advocates are trying to change policy on a smaller scale.

Advocates must also reach out to local legislators. A state senator or representative has a wide area of content to make decisions on; topics range from transportation to tax laws to education. If the legislature has never worked in the field of early education, then a legislator probably does not understand the details of child-care infrastructure or how the programs operate. One benefit for child-care advocates is that in recent years, both Republicans and Democrats have become much more interested in the field of child care due to its drastic impact on the workforce. During the child-care closures associated with the COVID-19 pandemic, emergency responders and essential employees had a difficult time attending work unless reliable and safe child care was available in their communities. Now, the US Chamber of Commerce, economists, and key businesses are all concerned about the availability of child care, and when large businesses are worried about finding necessary workers, they reach out to their legislators to talk about the barriers they are facing. Legislators know that there is a child-care crisis within their states, but they may not understand the possible solutions to this problem.

Again, advocates may have a limited amount of time to discuss mixed delivery with elected officials, so they should have specific talking points ready to catch the interest of legislative members when there is an opportunity. Possible talking points for public officials include:

- There is not enough quality child care in the state for all the children who need it, and when parents do not have a safe place for their children, they leave the workforce to provide that care themselves.
- Child care does not have a stable financial model. It costs more to operate a child-care program than parents can afford, so centers lose money and eventually close.
- Child-care programs need additional sources of funding to stay open. When state-funded pre-K and Head Start programs partner with child-care programs, the child-care programs have the extra funding to stay open to the community and they can offer more services to the families who enroll.
- Public child-care services benefit from partnerships with private child care. By sending enrolled students to high-quality child-care programs, they do not have to make capital investments in new facilities and can use the staff members at the child-care programs that are already in the early education field.

Explaining how the private programs and the public funding sources both benefit from these partnerships can be a huge selling point for legislative members. It can also be very helpful to explain how a lack of consistent child care can damage the economy as a whole.

Along with elected officials, child-care advocates should hold these same conversations with their state child-care offices and departments of education. These offices typically write the regulations for how child care and public schools need to operate after the legislators pass laws. Changes in policy often require state departments to drastically increase their workloads; however, many state government branches are willing to take on these temporary increases in workload when they see that it will benefit the groups that they are serving. Advocates should show these state offices how other states have navigated these policies before them; no one wants to take on unnecessary work. If another state has well-written regulations on how a mixed-delivery system should work, other state governments may want to use them as a template for their own changes. This will reduce their own work, and it may help them avoid barriers that the other state has already resolved.

CONDUCTING A POLICY CAMPAIGN

Once advocates have educated key stakeholders in the state on what a mixed-delivery system is and how it can benefit everyone involved, the next step is to request policy around a mixed-delivery framework. Most states currently have policies that would allow the state-funded preschool system to partner with a private child-care program if necessary; however, there may not be consistency throughout the state on how mixed delivery is used. Private child-care programs may not receive an equitable stipend across the state for the same type of enrollment. Also, child-care programs in certain regions may want to participate in this type of partnership, but the public school system may not want to. If the mixed-delivery program is administered at the state level, then there can be equitable access to partnerships and funding for programs across the state.

A state-administered program will need laws, or at least regulations, that govern the program to make sure that it is a unified system and provides all areas of the state with the same type of supports. There are two different ways to implement a unified state system:

- Regulations that are written by the executive branch office and approved by the legislature
- A state law passed by the legislature that is written into regulation by the executive branch

This means that advocates can either start their efforts working with the state offices of education and child care or with the legislative branch.

If advocates start lobbying the executive branch offices, those offices already understand the child-care and state-funded preschool systems. They may be able to determine the best way to write the policies for a smooth merger of the two systems. Once the executive branch writes the new regulations, they must be sent to the legislative branch for review and approval before going into effect. On the other hand, if advocates start by lobbying the legislative branch on their ideas for mixed-delivery early education, the legislature can write a bill that is passed into law, and then the departments of education and child care must construct regulations based on that legislation. Remember that legislative members may not understand the intricacies of the early education field, so the bill may not be as definite as if an early education specialist constructed the content; remember also that the governor still can veto the bill. In either instance, the early education advocates will have to make sure that both the legislative branch and the executive branch (with state offices in education, child care, and the governor's office) understand the composition of mixed delivery and why it is important.

When advocates decide who they want to write the new policies, it is important to remember that regulations can be changed more easily than laws. That can be both a good and bad thing for a proposed change in policy. If a law is passed on the new content, then it will take another law to make updates to the policy if the state finds that there are complications in the original policy that need to be ironed out. At the same time, the law can make it harder to change the established mixed-delivery system when a change in leadership comes into office that may have slightly different political leanings. Regulations are much easier to change, but that is both a strength and a pitfall. Only a legislative committee is typically used to approve new regulations, and most states do not have specific limits on how frequently regulations can be updated.

Advocates also need to align and determine what they are lobbying for before they begin their campaign. If the vast majority of a state's early childhood education community is advocating for the same change, such as an expansion of mixed-delivery services with a requirement that all school systems use a certain percentage of their early childhood funding for mixed-delivery partnerships, then many members of the legislature are more likely to agree on the components of the bill because they believe their constituents are backing it. Because jumping from limited mixed-delivery partnerships to a full universal pre-K program can be a complicated strategy, many states first try to expand mixed-delivery eligibility with limited participation and then eventually ask for a full universal preschool system.

IMPLEMENTATION TIMELINE

The advocates' policy campaign also leads to determining an implementation timeline. Implementing a full universal pre-K program overnight is almost impossible, so many states set goals, such as a five-year plan to develop universal pre-K with eligibility for mixed-delivery preschool services growing each year. The plan may include steps such as:

- Increasing the income eligibility guidelines for state-funded preschool to include more families and requiring public schools to use 15 percent of their funding for mixed-delivery classrooms.
- Phasing out income eligibility requirements and eventually using age as the only eligibility requirement for enrollment. This may include using a lottery to distribute enrollment slots until overall state capacity is built up.
- Using the age of the child as the only eligibility requirement for state-funded preschool and making sure that each child who enrolled is offered a slot. To get above the 70 percent enrollment level for universal pre-K, state employees may go into underserved neighborhoods to make sure that all children and families know that they can enroll in the state's universal pre-K at no cost.

These may be goals that are eventually met over a five-to-ten-year period depending on the state's funding resources and the physical capacity to house all the children whose families are interested in universal pre-K. When the timeline is established, it needs to be realistic. Expectant families should not be left waiting on early education programs that are not available yet. Early childhood advocates can use a recommended timeline to help legislative members understand the amount of state funding that will be needed over time to plan state budgets in multi-year budget cycles. When advocates go to government officials with requests, the government agencies want data, costs, and timelines to determine if the project is realistic—something that an official can present to the full branch of government as a possible success for the administration. This is why advocates need to come prepared when speaking in private meetings or before legislative committees with their plans to improve the system. Make the plans as concrete as possible, and show how other states have been successful. These are the data points that can win conversations.

It is also important for early childhood advocates, specialists, educators, and even parents to show their passion and determination for this initiative when presenting this information to others.

America is facing a nationwide child-care crisis, and our children are those most at risk of losing quality early childhood classrooms. Our nation's parents are most at risk of losing their jobs if they can't find reliable child care. Our child-care providers are most at risk of losing their businesses if the nation cannot develop a more stable infrastructure. Our children with disabilities are at risk of falling further behind developmentally if they cannot get the resources they need to help them start kindergarten as prepared as possible. These are facts to be passionate about because the early childhood community understands the importance of the fight they are facing. It is key to bring forward the stories of parents, child-care providers, and business owners who have been affected by quality child care and by the lack of quality child care. These stories, added to the concrete data, can have a huge pull on a successful campaign for expanding mixed-delivery preschool. Whichever strategy advocates begin with, it is critical to act now to support the child-care industry and make sure that all children have access to the early education system they need.

REFERENCES AND RECOMMENDED READING

Abbott v. Burke 100 N.J. 269 (1985).

Afterschool Alliance. 2021. "America after 3 PM Core Findings." Afterschool Alliance. http://www.afterschoolalliance.org/AA3PM/

Alawsaj, Manal, Max Berman, Teuta Mujaj, and Kayla Rankin. 2023. *State Universal Pre-K Policies: Lessons from Florida, Oklahoma, and Vermont.* Rockefeller Institute of Government. https://rockinst.org/wp-content/uploads/2023/01/clps-state-level-universal-prek-programs.pdf

Alliance for Early Success. 2022. "What Is Universal Pre-K?" Alliance for Early Success. https://earlysuccess.org/what-is-universal-pre-k?gclid=CjwKCAjw_MqgBhAGEiwAnYOAeoGZaGyJzcWiWL9fkHBHJ1zqYU_BnGds805fZ-0krVXN3e5VbiynMehoCq3AQAvD_BwE

Banghart, Patti, Maya Cook, and Martha Zaslow. 2020. "Approaches to Providing Comprehensive Services in Early Head Start-Child Care Partnerships." Child Trends. https://www.childtrends.org/publications/approaches-to-providing-comprehensive-services-in-early-head-start-child-care-partnerships

Barnett, Steve, and Rebecca Gomez. 2016. "Universal Pre-K: What Does It Mean and Who Provides It?" National Institute for Early Education Research, Rutgers Graduate School of Education. https://nieer.org/2016/01/06/universal-pre-k-what-does-it-mean-and-who-provides-it

Belfield, Clive R. 2018. "The Economic Impacts of Insufficient Child Care on Working Families." Ready Nation and Council for a Strong America. https://strongnation.s3.amazonaws.com/documents/522/3c5cdb46-eda2-4723-9e8e-f20511cc9f0f.pdf

Child Care Aware of America. 2020. "Picking Up the Pieces: Building a Better Child Care System Post-Covid 19." Child Care Aware of America. https://www.childcareaware.org/picking-up-the-pieces/

Child Care Aware of America. 2022. "Demanding Change: Repairing Our Child Care System." Child Care Aware of America. https://www.childcareaware.org/demanding-change-repairing-our-child-care-system/

Child Care Technical Assistance Network. 2020. Addressing the Decreasing Number of Family Child Care Providers in the United States. https://childcareta.acf.hhs.gov/resource/addressing-decreasing-number-family-child-care-providers-united-states

Child Care Works 2018. "Mapping Infant-Toddler Child Care Supply and Demand." Child Care Aware of America. https://cdn2.hubspot.net/hubfs/3957809/social-suggested-images/Mapping%20Infant%20and%20Toddler%20Think%20Babies%20Brief.pdf

Coffey, Maureen. 2022. "Still Underpaid and Unequal." Center for American Progress. https://www.americanprogress.org/article/still-underpaid-and-unequal/

Cui, Jiashan, and Luke Natzke. 2021. "Early Childhood Program Participation: 2019." Institute of Education Sciences, National Center for Education Statistics, US Department of Education. https://nces.ed.gov/pubs2020/2020075REV.pdf

Dichter, Harriett, and Ashley LiBetti. 2021. *Improving Child Care Compensation Backgrounder 2021.* BUILD Initiative. https://buildinitiative.org/resource-library/backgrounder-on-compensation-in-child-care/

Early Care and Education Consortium. 2021. "A Mixed-Delivery System Is the Most Sustainable and Efficient Solution to Meet Policy Objectives." Early Care and Education Consortium. https://www.ececonsortium.org/wp-content/uploads/2021/07/ECEC-Solutions-Paper-Mixed-Delivery.pdf

Early Childhood Learning and Knowledge Center. 2023. "Office of Head Start (OHS)." Administration for Children and Families. https://eclkc.ohs.acf.hhs.gov/about-us/article/office-head-start-ohs

First Five Years Fund. 2022. "Early Head Start-Child Care Partnerships." First Five Years Fund. https://www.ffyf.org/issues/ehs-ccp/

Fisher, Philip. 2021. "Who Is Providing for the Child Care Providers?" Center for Translational Neuroscience, University of Oregon. https://static1.squarespace.com/static/5e7cf2f62c45da32f3c6065e/t/60f979d6e6d4d36da3abebde/1626962390564/who-is-providing-for-providers.pdf

Frank, Gillian, et al. 2021. "Progress and Peril: Child Care at a Crossroads." National Association for the Education of Young Children. https://www.naeyc.org/sites/default/files/globally-shared/downloads/PDFs/resources/blog/naeyc_july_2021_survey_progressperil_final.pdf

Friedman-Krauss, Allison, et al. 2022. *The State of Preschool 2021: State Preschool Yearbook.* The National Institute for Early Education Research, Rutgers Graduate School of Education. https://nieer.org/wp-content/uploads/2022/09/YB2021_Full_Report.pdf

Garver, Karin, et al. 2023. "State Preschool in a Mixed Delivery System: Lessons from Five States." Learning Policy Institute. https://doi.org/10.54300/387.446

Gray, Peter. 2021. "The Case Against Universal Preschool." *Psychology Today.* https://www.psychologytoday.com/us/blog/freedom-learn/202105/the-case-against-universal-preschool

Griffey, Emily. 2016. "Piece by Piece—Building a Mixed-Delivery Early Learning System in Virginia." Voices for Virginia's Children. https://vakids.org/our-news/blog/piece-by-piece-building-a-mixed-delivery-early-learning-system-in-virginia

Griffey, Emily. 2019. "Proof That Public-Private Partnerships Work—What Comes Next?" Voices for Virginia's Children. https://vakids.org/our-news/blog/proof-that-public-private-preschool-partnerships-work-what-comes-next

Goldberg, Emma. 2020. "The Pandemic's Setbacks for Working Moms." *The New York Times,* July 2. https://www.nytimes.com/2020/07/02/insider/virus-working-moms.html

Gould, Elise, and Hunter Blair. 2020. "Who's Paying Now? The Explicit and Implicit Cost of the Current Early Care and Education System." Economic Policy Institute. https://www.epi.org/publication/whos-paying-now-costs-of-the-current-ece-system/

Gustafsson-Wright, Emily, Katie Smith, and Sophie Gardiner. 2017. "Public-Private Partnerships in Early Childhood Development: The Role of Publicly Funded Private Provision." Center for Universal Education at Brookings. https://www.brookings.edu/wp-content/uploads/2017/12/ecd-public-private-partnerships-20171227.pdf

Harms, Thelma, Richard M. Clifford, and Debby Cryer. 2014. *Early Childhood Environment Rating Scale.* 3rd edition. New York: Teachers College Press.

Haspel, Elliot. 2022. "America's Child Care Equilibrium Has Shattered." *The Atlantic*, July 23. https://www.theatlantic.com/family/archive/2022/07/us-childcare-programs-expensive-underfunded/670927/

Herschander, Sara. 2022. "U.S. Child Care: Parents Can't Afford It and Workers Can't Afford to Live." Capital and Main. https://capitalandmain.com/u-s-child-care-parents-cant-afford-it-and-workers-cant-afford-to-live

HighScope Educational Research Foundation. 2019. *Preschool Program Quality Assessment-R*. Ypsilanti, MI: HighScope Press.

Hogan, Lauren. 2021. "Compensation Matters Most: How and Why States Should Use Child Care Relief Funding to Increase Compensation for the Early Childhood Education Workforce." National Association for the Education of Young Children. https://www.naeyc.org/sites/default/files/globally-shared/downloads/PDFs/resources/blog/compensation_matters_most.pdf

Huey, Marie. 2021. "How Mixed Delivery Builds Equity and Inclusion for Families." Think Small Blog. https://thinksmallblog.org/how-mixed-delivery-builds-equity-and-inclusion-for-families/

Kentucky Administrative Regulations, Division of Child Care. 2022. 922 KAR 2:160 Child Care Assistance Program. Kentucky Cabinet for Health and Family Services. https://apps.legislature.ky.gov/law/kar/titles/922/002/160/

Leonhardt, Megan. 2021. "Many Child Care Workers Don't Earn a Living Wage—And That Was the Case Even before the Pandemic." CNBC. https://www.cnbc.com/2021/02/24/child-care-workers-among-the-one-of-the-lowest-paid-occupations.html

Lieberman, Abbie. 2021. "True Mixed Delivery Pre-K Includes Family Child Care—But How?" New America. https://www.newamerica.org/education-policy/edcentral/fcc-universal-pre-k/

Loewenberg, Aaron. 2022. "Kentucky Gets Creative in Addressing Its Child Care Staffing Shortage." New America. https://www.newamerica.org/education-policy/edcentral/kentucky-gets-creative-in-addressing-its-child-care-staffing-shortage/

Mader, Jackie. 2022. "Finding Child Care Is Still Impossible for Many Parents." The Hechinger Report. https://hechingerreport.org/finding-child-care-is-still-impossible-for-many-parents/

McMillan, James H. 2004. *Classroom Assessment: Principles and Practice for Effective Instruction.* 3rd edition. Boston, MA: Allyn and Bacon.

Meek, Shantel E., and Walter S. Gilliam. 2016. "Expulsion and Suspension in Early Education as Matters of Social Justice and Health Equity." Discussion paper. https://cca-ct.org/wp-content/uploads/2020/11/Expulsion-and-Suspension-in-Early-Education-as-Matters-of-Social-Justice-and-Health-Equity.pdf

Miranda, Brenda. 2017. "Higher Staff-to-Child Ratios Threaten the Quality of Child Care." Child Trends. https://www.childtrends.org/higher-child-staff-ratios-threaten-quality-child-care#_ftn1

Mueller, Eleanor, and Sam Sutton. 2023. "How the Child Care Cliff Could Yank Back the Labor Market." Politico. https://www.politico.com/newsletters/morning-money/2023/08/21/how-the-child-care-cliff-could-yank-back-the-labor-market-00112021

National Association for the Education of Young Children. 2020. *Developmentally Appropriate Practice: A Position Statement of the National Association for the Education of Young Children.* https://www.naeyc.org/sites/default/files/globally-shared/downloads/PDFs/resources/position-statements/dap-statement_0.pdf

National Head Start Association. 2022. "Head Start United: Removing Barriers to Access for Children and Families." National Head Start Association. https://nhsa.org/resource/head-start-united/

National Institute for Early Education Research. 2021a. "NIEER Outlines Plan to Achieve Universal Preschool in the US." National Institute for Early Education Research, Rutgers Graduate School of Education. https://nieer.org/press-release/nieer-outlines-plan-to-achieve-universal-preschool-in-the-us

National Institute for Early Education Research. 2021b. "Positive Effects of Universal High-Quality Preschool Persist through 10th Grade." National Institute for Early Education Research, Rutgers Graduate School of Education. https://nieer.org/press-release/positive-effects-of-universal-high-quality-preschool-persist-through-10th-grade

Office of Child Care. 2012. "CCDF Final Regulations." Administration for Children and Families, US Department of Health and Human Services. https://www.acf.hhs.gov/occ/law-regulation/ccdf-final-regulations

Office of Child Care. 2014. "Child Care and Development Block Grant Act (CCDBG) of 2014: Plain Language Summary of Statutory Changes." Administration of Children and Families. https://www.acf.hhs.gov/occ/law-regulation/child-care-and-development-block-grant-act-ccdbg-2014-plain-language-summary

Office of Head Start. 2022. "About the Office of Head Start." Administration for Children and Families, US Department of Health and Human Services. https://www.acf.hhs.gov/ohs/about

Patrinos, Harry A. 2023. "Designing Effective Public-Private Partnerships in Education." World Bank Blogs. https://blogs.worldbank.org/education/designing-effective-public-private-partnerships-education

Policy Equity Group. 2023. "Universal Pre-K Only Works If States Also Stabilize Infant and Toddler Care; Otherwise, It Can Be Detrimental." Policy Equity Group. https://policyequity.com/universal-pre-k-only-works-if-states-also-stabilize-infant-and-toddler-care-otherwise-it-can-be-detrimental/#:~:text=The%20missing%20message%20is%20that,of%20Labor%20data%20available%20here

Reed, Sue, et al. 2019. "Head Start and State Preschool Partnerships: Lessons Learned from Preschool Development Grantees." *Promising Practices for Preschool Partnerships*. Preschool Development Grant TA Center. https://oese.ed.gov/files/2021/04/PDG_Promising-Practices-Brief_508.pdf

Sharrock, Emily, and Courtney Parkerson. 2020. "Equitable Compensation for the Child Care Workforce: Within Reach and Worth the Investment." Bank Street College of Education. https://educate.bankstreet.edu/cgi/viewcontent.cgi?article=1003&context=bsec

Smith, Linda, Megan Campbell, Sarah Tracey, and Arabella Pluta-Ehlers. 2019. "Early Head Start-Child Care Partnerships: Spotlighting Early Successes Across America." Bipartisan Policy Center. https://bipartisanpolicy.org/download/?file=/wp-content/uploads/2019/03/Early-Head-Start-Child-Care-Partnerships.pdf

Sullivan, Emily T. 2021. "The Unintended Consequences of Universal Preschool." EdSurge.com. https://www.edsurge.com/news/2021-05-10-the-unintended-consequences-of-universal-preschool

Thornton, Dalia, et al. 2020. "Unifying Framework for the Early Childhood Education Profession." Power to the Profession. https://powertotheprofession.org/wp-content/uploads/2020/03/Power-to-Profession-Framework-03312020-web.pdf

University of Washington. 2022. "What's the Difference between an IEP and a 504 Plan?" Do-It. https://www.washington.edu/doit/what-difference-between-iep-and-504-plan

Urban Institute. 2022. *An Implementation Study of the Early Childhood Educator Pay Equity Fund*. https://www.urban.org/projects/dc-child-care-policy-research-partnership/implementation-study-early-childhood-educator

US Bureau of Labor Statistics. 2018. "Occupational Employment and Wage Statistics, 39-9011 - Childcare Workers." Occupational Employment and Wage Statistics. https://www.bls.gov/oes/tables.htm

US Bureau of Labor Statistics. 2020. "Occupational Employment and Wage Statistics, 39-9011 - Childcare Workers." Occupational Employment and Wage Statistics. https://www.bls.gov/oes/current/oes399011.htm

US Chamber of Commerce Foundation. 2021. "Reimagining Our Child Care System." Center for Education and Workforce. https://www.uschamberfoundation.org/blog/post/re-imagining-our-child-care-system

US Department of Education. 2019. "Statute Chapter 33." *Individuals with Disabilities Education Act*. https://sites.ed.gov/idea/statute-chapter-33

US Department of Health and Human Services, Administration for Children and Families, Office of Head Start, National Center on Parent, Family, and Community Engagement. 2018. *Head Start Parent, Family, and Community Engagement Framework*. 2nd edition. Office of Head Start, National Center on Parent, Family, and Community Engagement.

US Department of Labor. 2022. "Americans with Disabilities Act." Disability Resources, US Department of Labor. https://www.dol.gov/general/topic/disability/ada

Vanover, Sarah T. 2016. "Family Preferences for Childcare in Central Kentucky." *Online Theses and Dissertations* 442. https://encompass.eku.edu/etd/442

Vanover, Sarah T. 2021. *America's Child-Care Crisis: Rethinking an Essential Business*. Lewisville, NC: Gryphon House.

Virginia Early Childhood Foundation. 2021. *Virginia's Mixed Delivery Grant Program: A Retrospective.* https://vecf.org/wp-content/uploads/2021/11/VECF-Mixed-Delivery-Retrospective-Final-.pdf

Weisenfeld, G. G., and Ellen Frede. 2021. "Including Family Child Care in State and City-Funded Pre-K Systems: Opportunities and Challenges." National Institute for Early Education Research. https://nieer.org/research-report/including-family-child-care-in-state-and-city-funded-pre-k-systems-opportunities-and-challenges

INDEX

A

Abbott Preschool Program, 73, 74
Abbott v. Burke, 73
absences, 123
access to child care
    benefits to business community, 2, 5
    for children with special needs, 34–36
    Early Head Start-Child Care Partnerships (EHS-CCP), 54–55
    Head Start/Early Head Start, 17–18, 23
    for infants and toddlers, 23, 33–34
    lack of, 2, 36
    mixed-delivery care, 38, 39–41, 43
    need for, 5–6
    state-funded preschool/private child-care partnerships, 59–60, 61–63
    state-funded preschools, 9–10, 11, 13–14
    universal pre-K, 81–82, 85
accountability
    contract language about, 120, 128
    Head Start/Early Head Start, 16, 20–21
    Head Start/private child-care partnerships, 58
    state-funded preschool/private child-care partnerships, 65, 66
administrators, program
    Alabama mixed-delivery model, 68
    contractual obligations in partnerships, 124
    Florida mixed-delivery model, 70–71
    Head Start/private child-care partnerships, 56, 58
    Michigan mixed-delivery model, 71
    New Jersey mixed-delivery model, 73–74
    New York mixed-delivery model, 75
    professional development role, 99–101, 104
    state-funded preschool advocacy, 15
    West Virginia mixed-delivery model, 77–78
adult-to-child ratios/classroom sizes
    Early Head Start-Child Care Partnerships (EHS-CCP), 51, 52, 55
    Florida mixed-delivery model, 70
    as health and safety factor, 12, 30
    in infant and toddler private child-care, 31–32
    Michigan mixed-delivery model, 72
    New Jersey mixed-delivery model, 74
    New York mixed-delivery model, 76
    NIEER preschool benchmark about, 84
    Oklahoma mixed-delivery model, 77
    West Virginia mixed-delivery model, 78
advocacy, 131–37
    educating stakeholders, 131–34
    establishing implementation timeline, 136
    lobbying for policy, 134–35
Alabama Department of Early Childhood Education, Office of School Readiness, 68
Alabama Education Trust Fund, 69
Alabama mixed-delivery model, 68–70
Alliance for Early Success, 81
American Indian and Alaska Native Head Start, 18–19
Americans with Disabilities Act (ADA), 92
America's Child-Care Crisis: Rethinking an Essential Business (Vanover), 3
apprenticeships, 101–2, 110–11
assessments
    Alabama mixed-delivery model, 70
    contract language about, 124, 129

Head Start/Early Head Start, 20–21
Michigan mixed-delivery model, 72–73
New Jersey mixed-delivery model, 74–75
New York mixed-delivery model, 76
NIEER preschool quality benchmarks, 83–84
Power to the Profession recommendations, 103
private child-care programs, 31
West Virginia mixed-delivery model, 79

B

background checks, 29–30, 91, 125–26
benefits, employee, 111–13, 127
block grants, 26–28, 50, 61, 77, 127
business community, 2, 5

C

child abuse, 29, 30
Child and Adult Care Food Program (CACFP), 14, 53
Child Care and Development Block Grant (CCDBG), 26–28, 50, 61, 77, 127
child-care centers
    disadvantages of, 33, 40–41
    Early Head Start-Child Care Partnerships (EHS-CCP), 50–52, 56
    funding of, 6
    Head Start/Early Head Start, 18
    health and safety in, 29
child-care crisis, 1–7
    possible solutions, 3–7
    problems with current model, 1–2
child-care deserts, 2, 13, 36, 58
child-care market stabilization, 45–46
child-care providers
child-care subsidies
    Child Care and Development Block Grant (CCDBG), 26–28, 50, 61–63
    child-care assistance for child-care employees, 111–12
    insufficiency of, 6
    public-private partnerships and, 48
    state-subsidized child-care vs. state-funded preschool, 9
Classroom Assessment scoring tool, 70, 73, 124
classroom health and safety, 12, 29–30, 53–54
classroom sizes/adult-to-child ratios
    Early Head Start-Child Care Partnerships (EHS-CCP), 51, 52, 55
    Florida mixed-delivery model, 70
    as health and safety factor, 12, 30
    in infant and toddler private child-care, 31–32
    Michigan mixed-delivery model, 72
    New Jersey mixed-delivery model, 74
    New York mixed-delivery model, 76
    NIEER preschool benchmarks, 84
    Oklahoma mixed-delivery model, 77
    West Virginia mixed-delivery model, 78
coaching, 101–2
confidentiality, 129
contracts, 121–30
    defining key terms in, 122–23
    financial management, 127–28
    partners' obligations, 123–25
    performance evaluation, 129
    record-keeping and confidentiality, 128–29
    staff requirements, 125–27
    state-funded preschool/private child-care partnerships, 66
    terms/renewability/termination, 130
County Collaborative Early Childhood Core Team, 78

D

Designation Renewal System (DRS), 16
developmentally appropriate practices, 88–89
diversity, 45, 64
documentation, 128–29

E

early childhood education framework, 102–5

Early Childhood Environmental Rating Scale, 70, 124

Early Head Start. See Head Start/Early Head Start

Early Head Start-Child Care Partnerships (EHS-CCP)
- benefits, 54–57
- challenges, 57–58
- funding, 50–51
- quality components, 52–54

eligibility requirements
- Alabama mixed-delivery model, 69
- child-care subsidies, 27
- contract language about, 122
- Head Start/Early Head Start, 17–18
- Michigan mixed-delivery model, 71
- New Jersey mixed-delivery model, 73
- New York mixed-delivery model, 75
- Oklahoma mixed-delivery model, 77
- state-funded preschools, 11, 13–14
- universal pre-K, 81–83, 85, 136
- West Virginia mixed-delivery model, 77

emergency management plans, 30

enrollment, 42–43, 57, 128–29

equity, 5–6, 43, 107

F

facility and maintenance requirements, 124–25

families
- child care choice, 41–42, 55, 63–64, 89–90
- child-care market stabilization and, 45–46
- IEPs, rights regarding, 94–95
- scheduling needs of, 12–13, 23, 33, 39–41, 54–55, 89–90

family and community engagement, 21–22, 54

family care service, 19

family child-care homes
- benefits of, 4–5, 33, 36, 40–41, 89–90
- Early Head Start-Child Care Partnerships (EHS-CCP), 50–52, 56
- funding of, 6
- Head Start/Early Head Start, 18
- health and safety in, 29

Federal Education Rights and Privacy Act (FERPA), 94, 95

First Class Pre-K (FCPK), 68, 69–70

504 plan, 93

Florida mixed-delivery model, 70–71

Free and Appropriate Public Education (FAPE), 93, 94

funding
- Alabama mixed-delivery model, 68–69
- contract language about, 126–28
- documentation of, 58
- Early Head Start-Child Care Partnerships (EHS-CCP), 50–51, 56
- Florida mixed-delivery model, 71
- Head Start/Early Head Start, 16–17
- Michigan mixed-delivery model, 72
- mixed-delivery care, 39, 44, 105
- New Jersey mixed-delivery model, 74
- New York mixed-delivery model, 76
- Oklahoma mixed-delivery model, 77
- private child-care programs, 25–28, 31–32
- state-funded preschools, 11, 15
- universal pre-K, 88
- West Virginia mixed-delivery model, 78

G

Great Start Readiness Program (GSRP), 71–73

H

Head Start/Early Head Start, 16–24
- accountability procedures, 20–21
- eligibility, 17–18

establishment of, 16
family and community engagement, 21–22
funding, 16–17
marketing challenges, 24
scheduling challenges, 23
staffing, 19–20, 23–24
transportation challenges, 22
types of services, 18–19

Head Start Parent, Family, and Community Engagement Framework, 21
Head Start/private child-care partnerships, 49–50
Head Start Program Performance Standards (HSPPS), 19–20, 49, 52, 53, 57
health and safety, 12, 29–30, 53–54
health care benefits, employee, 112–13
health services (physical and mental), 53
home-based care, 18

I

inclusion, 43
Individual Family Service Plan (IFSP), 93, 94, 95
Individualized Education Plan (IEP), 93–96
Individuals with Disabilities Education Act (IDEA), 11, 93–96
   infant and toddler care
      access to, 23, 33–34
      adult-to-child ratios for, 31–32, 52
      employee compensation for, 33, 86–87, 107, 109, 110
      family child-care homes and, 4
      financial loss from, 45
      impact of universal pre-K on, 87
      special education mandates for, 93
inspections, 49, 124
insurance, 107, 111, 112–13, 125, 127

J

Johnson, Lyndon B., 16

K

Kentucky Administrative Regulations, Division of Child Care, 111–12
Kentucky child-care assistance program, 111–12

L

licensing, 49, 57, 103–4, 124

M

medications, administration of, 30
mental health services, 53
mentoring, 101–2
Michigan Department of Education, Office of Preschool and Out-of-School Time Learning, 71
Michigan Intermediate School Districts (ISDs), 71–73
Michigan mixed-delivery model, 71–73
Migrant and Seasonal Head Start, 18
mixed-delivery care, 37–47
   benefits for children, 46–47
   benefits to families, 39–42, 89
   benefits to private child-care programs, 44–46
   benefits to public schools, 42–44
   components of, 38–39
   examples of, 37–38
mixed-delivery care, planning and implementation, 114–20
   formal partnership agreement, 120
   goal development, 119–20
   implementation decisions, 79–80
   needs assessment, 115
   stakeholders, identification of, 115–17
   vision statement, 118–19
mixed-delivery care, state models, 67–80
   Alabama, 68–70
   Florida, 70–71
   Michigan, 71–73
   New Jersey, 73–75

Oklahoma, 76–77
West Virginia, 77–79

N

National Association for Family Child Care, 103
National Background Check Program, 91, 125
National Institute for Early Education Research (NIEER)
    quality benchmarks, 10, 11–12, 14, 83–84
    state-funded preschool definition, 8–9
    The State of Preschool 2021 report, 9–10, 12, 15, 82
    universal pre-K, 82, 85
New Jersey Department of Education, 73
New Jersey mixed-delivery model, 73–75
    New York Department of Education, Office of Early Learning, 75, 76
New York mixed-delivery model, 75–76
New York Quality Assurance Protocol, 76
NIEER (National Institute for Early Education Research)
    quality benchmarks, 10, 11–12, 14, 83–84
    state-funded preschool definition, 8–9
    The State of Preschool 2021 report, 9–10, 12, 15, 82
    universal pre-K, 82, 85
nursing profession model, 102

O

Obama, Barack, 50
Office of Child Care, 30
Office of Head Start, 20–21, 50
Oklahoma Academic Standards, 77
Oklahoma mixed-delivery model, 76–77
Oklahoma Standards for Accreditation, 77

P

partnerships, public-private, 48–66
    about, 48–49
    Early Head Start-Child Care (EHS-CCP), 50–58
    Head Start/private child-care, 49–50
    state-funded preschool/private child-care, 59–66
pay parity, 106–13
    arguments for, 3–4, 15, 86–87
    child-care assistance, 111–12
    problems with poor compensation, 106–8
    subsidizing employee health care, 112–13
    wages and benefits, 69, 74, 77, 109–11
policies and regulations, 134–35
Power to the Profession framework, 103–5
Preschool Expansion Program, 73–75
private child-care programs, 25–36
    access to, 33–36
    diversity in, 45
    funding for, 25–28, 31–32
    health and safety in, 29–30
    IEP and IFSP implementation in, 94–97
    impact of universal pre-K on, 87
    QRIS assessment for, 31
    scheduling challenges, 33
    staffing, 28–29, 32–33
professional designations, 103–4
professional development, 98–105
    coaching and mentoring, 101–2
    early childhood education framework, 102–5
    for early childhood educators, 99–101
professional organizations, 104–5
Program Quality Assessment—R, 73

Q

QRIS (Quality Rating and Improvement System), 31, 70, 73, 74, 76, 124
quality benchmarks, 10, 11–12, 14, 83–84

R

record-keeping, 128–29
rural areas, child care in, 36

S

scheduling challenges
    Early Head Start-Child Care Partnerships (EHS-CCP), 54–55
    Head Start/Early Head Start, 23
    mixed-delivery care, 39–41
    private child-care programs, 33
    state-funded preschools, 12–13
    universal pre-K, 89–90
special education, 91–97
    Americans with Disabilities Act (ADA), 92
    Individuals with Disabilities Education Act (IDEA), 11, 93–96
    mixed-delivery care, 44–45, 46–47
    public-private partnerships, 48–49
special needs, children with
    child care available for, 5–6
    Florida mixed-delivery model, 70
    mixed delivery care, 44–45, 46–47
    private child-care programs, 34–36
    public-private partnerships, 48–49
    state-funded preschools, 9, 11
staff compensation
    Alabama mixed-delivery model, 69
    arguments for parity in, 3–4, 15, 86–87
    benefits, 111–13, 127
    contract language about, 126–27
    Early Head Start-Child Care Partnerships (EHS-CCP), 55
    Head Start/Early Head Start, 23–24
    Michigan mixed-delivery model, 72
    New Jersey mixed-delivery model, 74
    New York mixed-delivery model, 76
    Oklahoma mixed-delivery model, 77
    Power to the Profession recommendation for, 104
    private child-care programs, 28, 32–33
    problems of, 106–8
    wage increases, 109–10
    West Virginia mixed-delivery model, 78–79
staffing challenges
    Early Head Start-Child Care Partnerships (EHS-CCP), 58
    Head Start/Early Head Start, 23–24
    private child-care programs, 28–29, 32–33
    state-funded preschools, 14–15
    universal pre-K, 86–87
staff shortages
    bus drivers, 22
    compensation, impact of, 24, 56, 107–8
    qualified teachers, 14–15, 23
staff training/education
    Alabama mixed-delivery model, 69
    coaching and mentoring, 101–2
    contract language about, 126
    Early Head Start-Child Care Partnerships (EHS-CCP), 52, 55
    Florida mixed-delivery model, 70
    Head Start/Early Head Start, 19–20
    Michigan mixed-delivery model, 72
    New Jersey mixed-delivery model, 74
    New York mixed-delivery model, 76
    Oklahoma mixed-delivery model, 77
    Power to the Profession recommendations, 102–5
    private child-care programs, 29
    professional development, 99–101
    state-funded preschools, 14–15
    West Virginia mixed-delivery model, 78
state child-care/education offices, 134–35
state-funded preschool/private child-care partnerships

arguments for, 59–61

challenges, 64–66

funding, 61–63

purposes, 63–64

state-funded preschools, 8–15

eligibility and access, 9–10, 11, 13–14

funding, 11, 15

lack of choice in, 41–42

quality of, 10, 11–12

scheduling challenges, 12–13

staffing challenges, 14–15

state legislators, 133–35

The State of Preschool 2021 report (NIEER), 9–10, 12, 15, 82

Statewide Universal Full-Day Prekindergarten (SUFDPK), 75–76

subsidies, child-care

Child Care and Development Block Grant (CCDBG), 26–28, 50, 61–63

child-care assistance for child-care employees, 111–12

insufficiency of, 6

public-private partnerships and, 48

substitute teachers, 111

T

transportation, 22, 125

tuition, private child-care, 26

U

universal pre-K, 81–90

developmentally appropriate practice, 88–89

funding challenges, 88

high-quality benchmarks, 83–84

impact on private child care, 87

implementation timeline, 136

NIEER plan for, 85

scheduling challenges, 89–90

staffing challenges, 86–87

US Department of Health and Human Services (HHS), 16, 50

V

Voluntary Prekindergarten Education Program (VPK), 70–71

W

wages, competitive

arguments for, 3–4, 15, 86–87

efforts to establish, 109–10

wage-supplement programs, 3

West Virginia Department of Education, Division of Teaching and Learning, 77

West Virginia mixed-delivery model, 77–79

West Virginia Pre-K Health and Safety Checklist, 79

West Virginia Pre-K Steering Team, 77

wrap-around services, 50, 55, 123

Y

Yale University Child Development Center, 49

Z

Zero to Three, 103